THE BIBLE
SPEAKS TO
OUR TIMES

ALAN REDPATH

THE BIBLE SPEAKS TO OUR TIMES

THE CHRISTIAN'S VICTORY IN CHRIST

Fleming H. Revell
A Division of Baker Book House Co
Grand Rapids, Michigan 49516

Published by Fleming H. Revell,
a division of Baker Book House Company
P.O. Box 6287, Grand Rapids, Michigan 49516-6287

ISBN: 0-8007-5492-1

Second printing, June 1998

Printed in the United States of America

For current information about all releases from Baker Book House,
visit our web site:
                    http://www.bakerbooks.com

PREFACE

While there is no special sequence of teaching in the chapters of this book, I trust the reader will recognize that there is a unity of message which runs through them. The Bible speaks to our times on every issue of the day, and within these pages are just a few matters concerning which God has burdened my heart.

The contents of this book have formed the subject of messages preached in recent years either from the pulpit of Moody Church, Chicago, or Charlotte Chapel, Edinburgh; and to the congregations of these churches I owe a great debt for their loving patience with a very inadequate ministry. It is my fervent prayer that as these messages appear in printed form the blessing of God may yet rest upon them, and so they may be the means of making a measure of Holy Spirit impact upon some.

To the American edition of this book I have added two further chapters on what I believe are tremendously important and practical subjects in the life of the church and the individual Christian today. Beset as we are by all kinds of Satanic attacks on evangelical Christianity, we need a clear-sounding note on the subject of Christian victory in the face of all these pressures.

In my judgment, there is no chapter in all the Bible which states this more clearly, and with no ambiguity whatever, than Romans 6, for here we are brought face to face with the Christian's identity with Christ in His death and resurrection. Far too many of us have dismissed this chapter from our minds because we have said that in experience it does not work, or because we have not understood it. In any case, we have thought such teaching was purely "judicial" or "positional."

No! This is the basic position in which the Christian finds himself from the very start of his experience of the grace of God: in complete victory in Christ. This is a position which the devil will assail right and left, but all he can do is persuade us to believe that it is not true, or that it is too high to attain. The truth is that it is not a matter of attainment at all. It is rather one of receiving what our wonderful Saviour has already accomplished for us. The Christian fights not *toward* victory, but *from* it.

I commend this chapter, and its counterpart on the subject of "Enemy Tactics in the Christian Warfare," to the careful consideration of every reader.

The style is very much that of preaching, so I trust for the forbearance of the critic who looks for greater precision in writing. May the fire which burnt in my heart when these messages were preached somehow be communicated through the printed page to all who read—and to Him by whose grace alone one is permitted to be in the ministry, be all the glory.

ALAN REDPATH

CONTENTS

The Bible Speaks to Our Times

1

THE VICTORY OF LOVE

. . . the Lord added to the church daily such as should be saved—ACTS 2:47

This chapter in the Acts of the Apostles has witnessed the birth of the most amazing society the world has ever known. It was without a directorate; it had no committees; it had not the gift of talented leadership; it was composed in the main of unschooled and unlettered men. It was without financial resources; it was born amidst hostile people who could command great material power which ought easily to have been able to crush it.

QUALITY

Yet around this society was centered all the hopes of God the Father, Son and Holy Spirit, insofar as they were concerned in the fulfillment of His purposes for the world. For the formation of this society He had given Himself, and now He had come to live in the heart of every single member of it, that He might be Director, Controller, Counselor and Guide. If His hopes are not to be disappointed, if His purposes are not to be frustrated, what would you consider must be the supreme quality which this society, His church, must possess? Let us answer that question by asking another. What quality was lacking in the lives of those through whom God had been working in fulfilling His purposes prior to the day of Pentecost? Where had man failed?

Consider the language of the Old Testament. "Thou

shalt love the Lord thy God with all thy heart, and with all thy soul, and with all thy strength, and with all thy mind, and thy neighbor as thyself." This was the chief commandment, and in this man had failed, for he forsook the Lord and loved other gods. Consider the language of the Gospels, and in particular the words of our Lord in the high-priestly prayer of John 17:21, "That they all may be one; as thou, Father, art in me, and I in thee . . . that the world may believe that thou hast sent me." Think again of the final question put to Peter around the breakfast table on the seashore—"Simon, son of Jonas, lovest thou me?" (JOHN 21:15).

Then consider the language of the New Testament and the sequel to Pentecost. Hear Paul speak (GALATIANS 5:22): ". . . the fruit of the Spirit is love"; I Corinthians 13:1: . . . "Though I speak with the tongues of men and of angels, and have not love, I am become as sounding brass, or a tinkling cymbal." Hear Peter speak: ". . . add to your faith . . . love" (II PETER 1:5); and I Peter 4:8: ". . . above all things have fervent love among yourselves: for love shall cover the multitude of sins." Hear John's testimony: "Beloved, let us love one another: for love is of God; and every one that loveth is born of God, and knoweth God. He that loveth not knoweth not God; for God is love" (I JOHN 4:7-8).

Yes! Pentecost marked the entrance into the world of this new society, the church, the body of Christ; and the secret of its victory—the only secret—is the new principle of love which must constrain it. With the coming of the Holy Spirit, the love of God is shed abroad in our hearts by the Holy Spirit which is given to us—Romans 5:5—and the influence which the church and every believer is to exercise upon the world is governed not by the degree of his or her intellectual ability, but by the measure of Holy Ghost love in the heart of every disciple. Other gifts have their place, but this is supreme.

Remember, the word "love" is not a patronizing affection, not mere courtesy or affability, but the same word which is used in relation to the love of God for the world in John 3:16. It is a love which hurts; a love which costs; a love which gives all. Who can define it? We can only gaze upon Calvary and from our hearts say:

> O 'twas love, 'twas wondrous love,
> The love of God for me;
> The love that brought my Saviour down,
> To die on Calvary.

It is that love which is the firstfruit of the Spirit, and therefore we would expect to see it in operation immediately after Pentecost, after the coming of the One who brought it to men's hearts; and, furthermore, we should feel the effect of it upon the world. That is exactly what we do see in Acts 2.

CHARACTERISTICS

Notice, then, *the characteristics of this church:* "They continued stedfastly in the apostles' doctrine" (ACTS 2:42). That means *love for the Word of God.* They went back to it again and again. "They continued . . . in fellowship"—that means *love one for another.* They "had all things in common" (v. 44)—they were together, in a "togetherness" which meant the sharing of the divine nature of the Lord Jesus and which was expressed in a great love the one for the other. "They continued . . . in the breaking of bread" (v. 42)—that meant *love for their Lord;* and they continued "in prayers," which simply meant *love for the place of prayer.* One cannot read these verses without being convinced that this was the force which mastered them in every relationship. The church must have this or perish. Indeed, there is no place in the church for anyone without it. Insofar as the quality of love masters your life and mine, so far will we have power to communicate the message of the Gospel to others.

CONSEQUENCES

Observe, then, *the consequences upon the world.* These appear to have been twofold, for when the love of God was shed abroad by the Holy Spirit in and through the early church, something happened on earth and something happened in heaven. Notice verse 43: ". . . fear came upon every soul. . . ." A church to be feared! That sense of awe which grips the heart of an unbeliever in the presence of a Spirit-filled Christian; that sense of the majesty of the presence of God which should meet the stranger who comes within our gates; that sense of His holiness which should forbid all unreality in our worship and which must demand sincerity as we meet in His presence. A sense of fear.

Then, again, notice verse 47: ". . . having favour with all the people." Fear and favor! What a strange combination, and yet how wonderful! A church so filled with the Holy Spirit does not have to seek the patronage of the multitude. That is what most of our churches are trying to do today—desperately attempting by any means imaginable to secure the patronage of people. Spending our time running after unconverted people who spend their time running away from us. What a declaration this is of the loss of Holy Spirit power. What a tragedy when we seek to find some substitute for the Holy Ghost. But when the love of God is shed abroad in our hearts by the Spirit, a believer reveals Christ in such a way that He becomes an attraction to people. Depart from Him and we lose the crowd, because we lose the magnetism of the cross.

INFLUENCE

When the compassion of Christ, the life of Christ, and the beauty of Christ are revealed through every Christian who forms part of the church, then the weary, lonely, defeated and sad will begin to turn to us for comfort, for help, and to discover the secret of life in Christ. That kind of church has favor with the people. That is the influential church.

We use the term "influential" so often today to describe a church because of the kind of people who attend it or the amount of money it has in its treasury. These are the sort of things which give a church status in the eyes of other people. But that is not influence in the New Testament sense of the word. Indeed, it is just the reverse. True influence is the drawing power of the love of God shed abroad in our hearts by the Holy Spirit. A church from which suspicion, mistrust, lack of confidence, coldness of heart have departed and have been replaced by love. A church which brings fear and favor.

Notice, also, that something happens in heaven (v. 47): ". . . the Lord added to the church daily such as should be saved." Yes, they were added to the church, but primarily to the Lord Himself. He did it. It was not their eloquence nor their efficiency, but the Lord who did it. And He will do it yet, if the same marks of love are on us.

ACTION

As you read this message, maybe the Holy Spirit has spoken to you as to how you can take action to make this glorious experience real. Love for the Word of God; love for our fellow Christians; and above all, love for the Lord Himself. Are these things the characteristic experience of your life? If not, ask God to make them so; and then, having asked Him, take action. Seek God in His Word every day. Let that be the first thing above all in your life. Seek to repair a break of fellowship with another Christian wherever it may exist by revealing the love of Christ in your heart to that person.

Take action and then echo the words of Charles Wesley —and pray:

> O Thou, who camest from above
>   The pure celestial fire to impart,
> Kindle a flame of sacred love
>   On the mean altar of my heart.

2

EXAMINE YOUR PRIORITIES

Peter, filled with the Holy Ghost, said . . .
—ACTS 4:8

I want to assume that you who read this chapter are a member of a local church or assembly. (If you are a Christian and you are not a church member, then you are out of the will of God!) On this assumption, let me ask you a question: What is your vision for the fellowship of which you are a member? What is your goal? What are you aiming at? The Scripture tells us that where there is no vision, the people perish; therefore I ask: As one who contributes to the fellowship of the church, what is your vision for it?

You know, it is perfectly possible to keep a church going, apart from the Holy Spirit! With ordinary common sense you may get quite a good crowd. By good organizing and carefully planned methods, you may even pack the church to capacity and—let me say it gently but firmly—you can even have a crowded evangelistic meeting! Yes, you may have enough money to carry on the work. It needs no divine unction on the part of the minister, evangelist or church member to achieve these objectives by themselves. In fact, you have only to go inside many of our churches to discover in a very few moments that they are little more than social clubs with a Sunday service added.

I remember, some time ago, a church bulletin board advertising coming events. On one side of the board there was a statement—"Be sure to come to the Autumn Bridge

Party and Dance." On the other side—"It is not too early to join our Christmas Club and Bazaar." And right in the middle of the notice board—would you believe it?—the subject for the Sunday morning sermon was announced as "The Lost Radiance"! It would not have taken more than a few moments' conversation to suggest respectfully where the radiance had been lost.

But then, of course, you would say, "But my church is not like that. We have a name. We want to reach out to the neighborhood and win people for Christ. We want to see the influence of our fellowship extended. Indeed, our slogan is 'Evangelize or perish!'" Stop a minute. That is splendid. The very suggestion that your church could have any less vision than that has horrified you. You want it to be a New Testament church, founded on New Testament teaching, with a New Testament vision. Excellent! But may I ask you this twofold question: What are *you doing?* Or perhaps, deeper than that: What are *you being* to see that the vision is achieved? Just suppose that every other Christian in your fellowship were like you. Would that vision which you say is yours be accelerated or retarded in its achievement? Just think that out for a moment.

Now turn to the Word of God and look at the fourth chapter of the Acts of the Apostles. Consider the vision of the New Testament church and how it became real in experience.

THE OPPOSITION TO BE FACED

The apostles were face to face with powerful enemies. The center and focal point of opposition was not the Pharisees so much as the Sadducees, who were "grieved that they taught . . . through Jesus the resurrection from the dead" (v. 2). The opposition were purely materialistic in their outlook. They denied the supernatural. They explained away every miracle. In a word, they were first-century Modernists, and the conflict between them and the church was inevitable, and one or the other must die.

Basically, this is the very situation which confronts the evangelical church today. And before we even think of our vision, it is vital to understand where our center of opposition lies. If we say we want to evangelize and to take our stand on New Testament teaching, then there must be a clash. If you want a New Testament church, based on New Testament teaching, with New Testament fruit, that means you believe that a man who has not closed with God's offer of salvation in Christ is bound for a Christless eternity; in other words, that he is lost and that he needs saving.

When you read John 3:16, the most gripping words in it are *"should not perish."* That being so, your whole church life is regulated by this urgent factor; and the whole ministry, from pulpit and membership, is inspired by the urge which the knowledge of the need of a man without Christ creates; and that church rises up as one unit to war, to preach, to exhort and to save. At once there is a clash— not primarily with the humanism, rationalism and liberalism of this generation, which insists that such beliefs as these are totally out of date and disproved by everything that goes in the name of scientific progress and evolution.

On this issue there can be no compromise, for it all centers upon our attitude to the Word of God. We may have some differences of view as to what we mean by the inspiration of the Bible, but we know it not as a Book to be criticized, but as one which criticizes us—as a Book which is utterly and completely authoritative and God-breathed. We may not understand it all, but if God is small enough to be understood, He can scarcely be great enough to be worshiped; and therefore, as John Newton once said, "I will put down all apparent inconsistencies in the Bible to my own ignorance." To accept this viewpoint of the Word is to have a message that burns in our hearts for the day in which we live. To reject it means that we have no message at all.

THE OBJECT WE MUST ACHIEVE

In defiance of the opposition they encountered, Peter and John returned to their own company and prayer: "Lord, behold their threatenings: and grant unto thy servants, that with all boldness they may speak thy word, By stretching forth thine hand to heal; and that signs and wonders may be done by the name of thy holy child Jesus" (ACTS 4:29-30). Notice that they did not ask for the opposition to cease, but they did ask for courage to speak the Word of God and that their speaking should be accompanied by the Saviour's delivering power.

Yes, that was their passion—signs and wonders. Indeed, it was their only hope of success. It was the only thing which could silence the enemy. What a wonderful verse is the fourteenth verse of this chapter: ". . . beholding the man which was healed standing with them, they could say nothing against it." Of course, they could not. That man was not asked to give his testimony. It was sufficient that he was *standing,* a thing he had not been able to do all his life.

The church has no grip on the world unless through its

ministry men are being spiritually healed and delivered. That is why our grip has been lost. This kind of thing is just not happening. The final unassailable answer of the church is not merely the conversion of a soul, but the making of a disciple, and if we are to face the materialism of today, the rationalism and unbelief, the denial of the supernatural, we must have these evidences. It is no use arguing if we have not got them. Our object must be souls, men and women whose lives are transformed; and if we are not getting them, no amount of evangelical orthodoxy will avail. The world has every right to say to us, "Produce your credentials." Oh, if only you and I could speak with a man delivered standing by our side!

Let me now ask you this question: What are *you doing* about it? If everybody in your fellowship did as much for the Lord or talked as much about Him as you do, where would your church be in a year's time? That is a question which none of us can escape.

THE SECRET OF SUCCESS

". . . they . . . perceived that they were unlearned and ignorant men," but "they took knowledge of them, that they had been with Jesus" (v. 13). You realize, do you not, that in one sense the people who made that statement about the disciples were wrong? You see, they were Sadducees. They did not believe in a risen Christ. They imagined that, having crucified Him, they had finished with Him, and they were simply saying that these men seemed to be like Jesus because they had walked with Him and talked with Him and been close company for two or three years during His lifetime. That would not worry the Sadducees unduly because the effect of such a lingering contact would no doubt disappear in time. But they were wrong. The truth was that the similarity of the disciples to Christ was due to a daily, intimate contact with a living and ever-present Saviour. "Peter, filled with the Holy Ghost, said . . ." (v. 8).

COMMUNION WITH THE HOLY SPIRIT

Ah, that is it! Companying with Jesus on a roadside had not transformed the disciples, but communion with the Holy Spirit as Lord in their hearts had done so. This is the church's only hope—the Holy Ghost in fullness; and the privilege of that companionship is yours—in the kitchen, in the home, in the office, wherever you are—and it is that which produces inevitably a character which is Christlike. ". . . we all, . . . beholding as in a glass the glory of the Lord, are changed into the same image" (II CORINTHIANS 3:18).

How often we hear people say of the Christian, "If that is Christianity, I have no use for it." What a wonderful thing it would be if instead we were to hear them say something like this: "Have you met Mr. X lately? Do you remember how self-assertive he used to be? He isn't like that now. He has become so humble and gracious. He must have been with Jesus." Or: "Do you remember Mrs. Y? How critical she was of others and how ready to speak unkindly? Why, she does not do that now. Her tongue is always kind and her speech is thoughtful. She must have been with Jesus."

Surely, that is our only hope. If you want a New Testament church, then you must be a New Testament Christian. You must live in the daily enjoyment of the fullness of His blessing; and if you do that, then you must show the Lord that you really care. And that brings us back to the most fundamental thing of all—our personal prayer life.

Are you keeping your appointment in the place of prayer regularly? If so, you will know what it is to be swept along by the power of the Spirit of God. Does it amaze you that so often you pray only because you are driven to it? How often the pressure of other duties—the care of children, the care of the home, school, examinations, work, a thousand and one things—crowd in and the disciplined prayer life is crowded out. There lies in your room somewhere the Bible that is neglected, the prayer list that is out of date, the prayer letters that are all confused and unread. That is the testing point of every life. To win the battle is to see the windows of heaven opened and the blessing outpoured. To lose it is to know the heavens become as brass, the ground as hard as iron, and at the end of life's journey surely the judgment of God will be pronounced upon the tragedy and the sin of our prayerless living.

What is your vision? What is your goal? Examine your priorities. Are they wrong? If so, do not allow another day to pass without seeing to it that they are adjusted, whatever may be the cost.

> Come in, oh, come! the door stands open now;
>   I knew Thy voice; Lord Jesus, it was Thou;
> The sun has set long since; the storms begin;
>   'Tis time for Thee, my Saviour, oh, come in!
>
> Come, not to find, but make this troubled heart
>   A dwelling worthy of Thee as Thou art;
> To chase the gloom, the terror, and the sin:
>   Come, all Thyself, yea, come, Lord Jesus, in!

3

THE MOST IMPORTANT QUESTION IN LIFE

*. . . he saith unto them, But whom say ye that
I am? And Peter answereth and saith unto him,
Thou art the Christ*—MARK 8:29

At the conclusion of Mark 8 we have one of the most unfortunate chapter divisions of the *King James Version*. There are several verses, and the *Revised Version* helps a bit by putting these in paragraphs. The first verse of Chapter 9 is really part of Chapter 8, and indeed is the climax to it all: ". . . he said unto them, Verily I say unto you, that there be some of them that stand here, which shall not taste of death, till they have seen the kingdom of God come with power."

The Lord Jesus came that He might set up a kingdom, not in finality (He is coming again to do that), but in power; and this He did less than twelve months after the words were spoken, when at Pentecost He gathered together a little group of men and women and the Spirit of God came upon them. There was set up then on earth a kingdom of redeemed humanity, men and women who had been redeemed by the blood of Christ and who now had incarnate within them the new nature, who were to challenge the world and to face humanity with the gospel until Jesus comes again.

For two thousand years, with greater or lesser activity and effect, this message has swept across the inhabited earth. The effect has always been greater when the principles of power, so clearly revealed in this passage we are about to study, have been observed. The times when the power of the gospel has been so ineffective have been very largely those in which the church has failed to appreciate and understand the only principles and channels along which power can flow.

In this particular passage of the Word of God, the time had come for the Lord Jesus to call for a verdict. The crowds were thronging around Him, and would very gladly have crowned Him king of a material kingdom. The rulers were becoming increasingly hostile and angry, and were bent on His murder. The disciples, caught in between those two lines of opinion, were confused and uncertain of themselves. So now we see the Lord Jesus in the last six months of His earthly ministry, moving toward a climax where He must receive from the people, and above all from His disciples, a verdict concerning Himself. So you have what I have called, in verses 27-29, *the Challenge to Decision.*

Jesus "asked his disciples, saying unto them, Whom do men say that I am? And they answered, John the Baptist: but some say, Elias; and others, One of the prophets. And he saith unto them, But whom say ye that I am?"

You notice He moves from the circumference to the center: "Whom do *men* say that I am?"; and then, "Whom do *ye* say that I am?" The answer concerning the viewpoint of men differed: John the Baptist, Elias, one of the prophets. Here I see a very clear picture of the confusion that exists in theological thinking today. In some areas we have perhaps forgotten that the Person of Jesus Christ is not merely at the heart of the Christian faith, but He *is* the Christian faith. Christianity is Christ, and the most important question with which everybody has to be faced through life is: What think ye of Christ?

Notice that the Lord Jesus did not say: "What do you think about what I said?" Or, "What do you think about what I've done?" Or, "What do you think about what I have taught?" His question was, "Who do you think I am?" On the lips of anybody else save Christ, this question would be utterly inappropriate; but on the lips of the Lord it seems perfectly natural as He constantly draws the attention of people away from everything, even His preaching, even His works, to Himself.

"Whom do men say that I am?" In theological circles today there is confusion because we have departed from this, and have considered, "What about His teaching? What about His works? What did He say, and what was the effect of it all?" Today you have a condition of absolute confusion, of shifting sand, with no solid bedrock concerning the Christian faith, and this is a very real danger. Such names, many of them perhaps familiar to you, as Brunner and Barth, two great theologians of this century, are beginning to pass into the background with their neo-orthodoxy, and they are being replaced by such as Bultmann, who has moved farther away toward the liberal position. But the world is going after them, and one by one they move to this or to that or to the other, and they find themselves on sinking sand.

Men need to be brought back, not to what they think about doctrine, but to what they think of the Lord Jesus Christ, the very heart of the message. He *is* the message. We live in a day of shifting, sinking sand, a day of uncertainty, a day of lack of real conviction in many areas of the Christian church.

The most important question of the Lord Jesus was not, "What do men say?" but, turning to the little group of disciples, "Whom do ye say that I am?" This was the great moment of their testing. They had walked and talked with Him for two years and more. They had watched Him at work. They had heard His messages. They had seen Him confront all His enemies, and they had seen His miracles. Now, as the outcome of all that, the Lord Jesus focuses the attention of these men and says: "Whom do ye say that I am?" Ah, this was the challenge to a verdict! This was the thing that mattered most. This was the thing upon which He was going to stake every part of their ministry throughout all the future.

The issue today is not what I think about His teaching, or His doctrine, or men's interpretation of it, but what do I make of the Lord Jesus Christ Himself? "Whom do *ye* say that I am?" Ask yourself—have you settled that question personally? If you have, have you understood the implications of what is involved in the settlement of such a question in relation to your own life?

This question is immediately followed by *the confession of the disciples:* "And Peter answereth and saith unto him, Thou art the Christ." That is not a name for Jesus. That is a title, and it means *Messiah, King, the Anointed One of God.* It is significant of absolute authority. I imagine Peter (of course, he was always the spokesman!) was probably speaking for the other eleven. Peter had looked into the face of our Lord; he had followed him so long that he had never-forgotten, memorable days in his own experience, none more memorable than that when he had been almost drowned in a lake, and the Lord rescued him and brought him back to the ship. Many such instances had convinced Peter, beyond any shadow of a doubt, that this One with whom he walked and talked was none other than the Messiah, the King, the Lord.

That is a wonderful confession from Simon Peter. It is

not recorded by Mark, but in Matthew 16:17 Jesus immediately replied to him, "Blessed art thou, Simon Bar-Jona:
for flesh and blood hath not revealed it unto thee, but my
Father which is in heaven." In other words, this man had
come to a particular conviction concerning Jesus, not by
his own probing or understanding, not by his own investi-
gation, but by a revelation from heaven.

Nobody, says the Scripture, can call Christ "Lord" except by the Holy Spirit (I CORINTHIANS 12:3). Therefore,
when a man suddenly gets right concerning his convictions regarding Jesus Christ, it is because heaven has
opened upon him; and into that man's heart and life has
come a strange but real conviction which nothing can
ever shatter, and which the years can never change, as he
has looked up into the face of the Lord Jesus and said,
"Thou art the Christ!" It has come not by his understanding, his education, nor his personal probings, but by a
shaft of light that the Spirit of God has shone into his
heart; and without any question of doubt he has confessed
the absolute Lordship of Jesus.

Jesus went on to say, ". . . and upon this rock [that is,
upon your confession of My sovereignty, upon your acknowledgment that I am the Messiah, upon your submission to My Lordship] I will build my church" (MATTHEW
16:18).

Lest we think the Lord Jesus is diverting from the
kingdom which He had come to build, I remind you that
the word for "church" is *ecclesia,* used in every Greek city
to denote civil authority: it was represented by the *ecclesia.* So the Lord is saying to Simon Peter, "I have heard
your confession and your convictions concerning Myself.
Whenever I find a man making that confession, absolutely
assured in his heart that I am the Lord, upon that rock

will I build My kingdom." For two thousand years the Lord Jesus has been doing this in the lives of the people who have made that confession, who have settled the issue concerning the personality of Jesus Christ, and who then have done something more: they have understood the implications of it.

The Lord is asking for a verdict, and He is facing you now, saying, "Whom do you say that I am?" Have you settled, beyond any shadow of a doubt, that He is the Christ, the Son of the living God? Then He would say, as He said to Simon: "Blessed art thou!" This is not something that you have understood by your intellectual attainment. It is something you have come to see because God has shone into your heart the reality of the Person and supremacy of Jesus Christ.

I imagine that thus far I have carried you with me. But I have a feeling that, before I go much further, I might lose some friends, and I may leave some behind, though I trust not.

Notice that as soon as the Lord Jesus received this confession from Simon Peter, He then began to do something that He had never done before (MARK 8:31-32): ". . . to teach them, that the Son of man must suffer many things, and be rejected of the elders, and of the chief priests, and scribes, and be killed, and after three days rise again. And he spake that saying openly"—which means "plainly," so that all could understand. For the first time in His ministry, having received the confession from His disciples and their conviction as to who He was, He then said concerning Himself some words which shook them to the core: He must suffer, He must be rejected, He must be killed, He must rise again and (in the last verse of this same chapter) He must come again.

For the first time our Lord revealed to them not only His Person but His program for all His followers, and His plan of salvation for the world. The Son of Man must— not, if you please, because He is the victim of circumstances or because the powers of the enemy are too strong for Him—suffer, and must be rejected, and must be killed and must rise again. He never speaks of the cross without the resurrection. He did not hope that one day He would get through, that one day there would be another life beyond the grave. Oh, no! He said the Son of Man must do these things and He must rise again. It was a word of absolute authority, which Simon Peter, who didn't understand it then, understood some months later, for in preaching on the day of Pentecost he said: "Him, being delivered by the determinate counsel and foreknowledge of God, ye have taken, and by wicked hands have crucified and slain" (ACTS 2:23). It was all in the plan, thought out from before the foundation of the world. This was no emergency nor crisis in which God had to think up something new. It had been the plan in the heart of God from the very beginning.

Look at some of the words Jesus used in these verses. He must "be rejected of the elders, and of the chief priests, and scribes": the elders, that is the civic authority; the chief priests, the religious authority; the scribes, the moral authority. In every area, all of this great power was arrayed against our Saviour. That was a new idea to those men; they had never thought of it. From their knowledge of the Old Testament, they would know about a messiah who would come to set up a kingdom. They would also know about one who would come and would suffer, but they had never connected the two as one person. The Lord had now convinced them that He is the One who must suffer, and be killed and rise again.

Then dear old Peter—just look at him in verse 32! I suppose, to save the Lord from the humiliation of a public rebuke from His disciples, Peter out of charity called Jesus aside and spoke to Him, as recorded in Matthew 16:22. Matthew tells us what Peter said to Jesus, and Mark tells us what Jesus said to Peter. Mark got his information from Peter, who was not ashamed to let Mark have the story of how the Lord rebuked him. But Matthew tells what Peter had to say to Jesus. Peter heard Christ unveil the program and said to Him, in effect, "Be it far from Thee. Not that way! Not the way of the cross!" You notice that Jesus turned His back on Peter, who had drawn Him aside, and faced all the other disciples, and rebuked him: "Get thee behind me, Satan: for thou savourest not the things that be of God, but the things that be of men" (MARK 8:33).

There is nothing the devil enjoys more than doing his work through Christian people. Here is Peter in a blaze of light concerning who Jesus is, but in absolute darkness concerning what Jesus is going to get done. In other words, concerning the Person, "Thou art the Christ!"; concerning the plan, "I don't know a thing about it, and I don't want it that way. I would rather have it another way. I want to be prime minister in the kingdom; I don't want the cross, the suffering and rejection. Lord, not that way; be it far from Thee!"

"Get thee behind me, Satan." Yes, Satan had said it personally to Him in the wilderness, implying: "Take all these kingdoms without the cross! Just bow before me in a moment's worship, and You can have them all!" And Jesus had said to him, "Thou shalt not tempt the Lord thy God" (MATTHEW 4:7).

Now the same voice spoke, if you please, through one of His disciples and said, "Lord, take the kingdom, but not that way!" And Jesus turned His back upon His disciple, faced the others, and said: "Get thee behind me, . . . thou savourest not the things that be of God, but the things that be of men."

Oh, that the Spirit of God might write this upon our hearts! I have talked about the shifting sands of our theology today, of neo-orthodoxy and liberalism. But I'll tell you something that grieves my heart still more, and I think it a far greater menace to the cause of Christ today than anything on earth, and far more serious. It is the tragedy of evangelicalism in our land, where so often we have the same clichés, the same formulas, the same methods as we had fifty years ago. Now, of course, I am well aware that the Word of God is absolute in its authority. But I have the deep conviction that one of the great problems is that there are so many of us who are right in regard to His Person, but wrong in regard to His program. I scarcely think there would be many but would look up into His face with me and say, "Lord Jesus, Thou art the Christ, the Son of the living God." With sincerity we believe it, and with all our heart we are sure who Jesus is. Ah, but when it comes to the plan of action, we are living in a different world from the one of fifty years ago. We live in a world which has the most serious threat in all its history to our civilization, and I believe the threat of communism can only be met by men and women who are not only convinced of Christ's Person, but who are submitted to His program.

Yet we say that the methods we had fifty years ago will do. And what is the matter with that formula of salvation? Teach people some texts, get some truths into their minds and heads, and then they'll profess conversion. Give them the formula, and then they'll be born again; and the same methods, the same way as in the beginning, is now and ever shall be! Brethren, the next step to a rut is a grave! Unless fundamentalism has a revival, it will be buried before we have a chance to recover; and there is no place we can have revival except where people are right in their appreciation of who Jesus is and are submitted to His program.

But if we are wrong in relation to His plan, we savor not the things that be of God, but the things that be of men. What about our pious testimony, and how does it fit alongside our general behavior? What about our lack of any sense of being in a spiritual warfare day and night, seven days a week? What about our comfort, our luxury, our indulgence? What about the way we can turn off the spiritual tap at the end of the meeting, and five minutes later play the fool? What about our behavior when we are off duty, on vacation, and not actually in the meeting or service? What about our carelessness? What about our lack of real travail in prayer? What about our lack of discipline?

There are two alternatives in this civilization now: either humanity will be submitted to the authority of communism, or it will be submitted to the authority of God. There is no halfway ground. Man must live under authority; that is his very nature. I tell you, one of the gravest perils to world history is on our very doorstep. Communism knows perfectly well that it hasn't got what the Christian church has, and it knows that the greatest menace to the spread of communism is the Christian church when it lives in revival, and that is the one thing it fears. The one thing that can hold back the scourge of communism is men and women who have submitted not only to the Person but to the plan of Jesus Christ, and have gone the way of the cross. I believe that our God looks down upon much of evangelical life and He says: "Thou savourest not the things that be of God, but the things that be of men," when He sees our lighthearted, superficial, casual playing church instead of being in a desperate crusade for death or life.

Well—so what? you say. The Lord Jesus unveiled to those men His program, with which His followers have to be identified. But then, will you please observe, *He called them to discipleship,* (vv. 34-38). How many times do I read "Whosoever"? Four times. It has been struck so deeply into my heart by the Spirit that I cannot shelter under the "whosoever" of John 3:16 and get out from the implications of Mark 8. I cannot say, ". . . whosoever believeth in him shall not perish, but have everlasting life," unless I am prepared to get into this other "whosoever" and not be ashamed of Him in this day and this generation.

What does Jesus say as He announces His program and calls to discipleship? "Whosoever [not a few, but *whosoever*] will come after me [that is, be My followers], let him deny himself [that is, leave himself behind altogether, no consideration of self any more], and take up his cross, and follow me." What a procession of crosses! We cannot take up Jesus' cross. He took it alone for my sin. He will not take up my cross. I have to take it, but He will give me strength to bear it.

There is a cross in every one of our lives; it involves the crucifixion of the flesh and the death of it all, that we might follow after the Lord. In my mind, I see a great procession which has gone on for two thousand years, headed by the Lord Jesus carrying the cross of Calvary. Each one has left self behind, and on each one's shoulder there is a cross which he is carrying, and the Lord is giving strength to bear it. What a procession!

Notice the two contrasting philosophies in verse 35: "For whosoever will save his life shall lose it; but whosoever shall lose his life for my sake and the gospel's, the same shall save it." Peter's philosophy (and that, so often, of ourselves) was, "Save your life!" "But you will lose it," says Jesus. Jesus' philosophy is, "Lose your life, and then you'll gain it." And you can't have the two. Cherish the material and the present, and you'll lose the future. Cherish the things that are eternal, and you'll forget about the present. "For"—and He gives us the hypothetical example in verse 36—"what shall it profit a man, if he shall gain the whole world, and lose his own soul?" I can't gain the whole world, nobody ever could; that is hypothesis. But even if I could gain a little or much of it and put it into the scale, the whole world is just like a little feather beside the weight of my soul which I have lost because I've lived for time instead of eternity. ". . . what shall a man give in exchange for his soul?" (v. 37). Of course, he can't buy it back again. He has given it to time, to material things, to the present, and has lost out for all eternity. He cannot buy it back; that is a sheer impossibility.

Then Jesus closes His word to the disciples, saying, "Whosoever therefore shall be ashamed of me and of my words in this adulterous and sinful generation; of him also shall the Son of man be ashamed, when he cometh in the glory of his Father with the holy angels" (v. 38). Our present attitude toward the Saviour decides His future attitude toward us. Time simply runs into eternity. *Now* and *then* are linked together. Every railway track leads to a terminal: it will get there: it is a terminal; it is inevitable. No coward here will be crowned in heaven. No one who has not accepted the principle of His program will ever stand accepted before the Lord Jesus. It is so amazing that He isn't ashamed of us, but it is even more amazing that we could ever be ashamed of Him.

Which of these ways of life is yours? To be able to say, "Thou art the Christ, the Son of the Living God," and to say it without any reservation at all; to be right about His Person is absolutely worthless for salvation if you are wrong about His plan—then "thou savourest not the things that be of God, but the things that be of men." I hope you see, on the one hand, the shifting sand of theology, and, on the other hand, the decadence around us which is right about Jesus but wrong about the program.

Have you submitted to Christ, but rejected the plan of the cross? Have you turned your back upon self and left it behind, and are you dedicated, abandoned completely to His plan in your life? That is not popular. It takes a lot of people off the fence theologically (alas, that some of them get off on the wrong side!), but I'm happy that people cannot be left on the fence in the face of what Jesus says today: "Whom say ye that I am?"

God grant that you may be right about the Saviour. Yes, He is the Christ. And God grant that you may be right, too, about the plan: "Whosoever will come after me, let him deny himself, and take up his cross, and follow me."

4

THE SIGNIFICANCE OF CHRISTMAS

Behold, a virgin shall be with child—MATTHEW
1:23

Matthew's account of the birth of our Lord is told so frankly, so simply, so beautifully. Chapter 1:23 underlines His birth as something which God had planned and timed perfectly, something that the people of Judah had anticipated, though only in a very limited sense. Quoting from Isaiah 7:14, Matthew says: "Behold, a virgin shall be with child, and shall bring forth a son, and they shall call his name Emmanuel, which being interpreted is, God with us." That was the hope of Israel.

In Isaiah 9:6 are written those tremendous words, ". . . unto us a child is born, unto us a son is given: and the government shall be upon his shoulder: and his name shall be called Wonderful, Counselor, The mighty God, The everlasting Father, The Prince of Peace." If you refer to Matthew 1:21, you find that Old Testament hope comes to realization: ". . . thou shalt call his name Jesus: for he shall save his people from their sins."

The hope of the people, *Emmanuel.* The answer of God, *Jesus.* The hope of the people, that somehow out of darkness God would come and deliver them from an outward tyranny, a human bondage. The answer of heaven, *Jesus:* ". . . he shall save his people from their sins." How much greater was heaven's answer than the hope of those people at that time!

You notice the Lord was never called "Emmanuel" in the New Testament. He never bore that name, though actually the meaning of it was often quoted in New Testament language. For instance, in the Gospel of John, which begins with such a majestic chord: "In the beginning was the Word, and the Word was with God, and the Word was God." Then, after a parenthesis, comes this statement: ". . . the Word was made flesh, and dwelt among us, (and we beheld his glory, the glory as of the only begotten of the Father,) full of grace and truth." God with us—*Emmanuel.*

The word "Jesus" somehow expresses, so much more completely than any Old Testament name ever could, the real purpose of the coming of our Saviour. Let us meditate about the hope that the people of Israel had as they anticipated His coming. All through the centuries the Jewish people had longed for someone to come and deliver them.

Matthew 1:17 is a summary of the genealogy of our Lord, and—those of you who may be inclined to be critical of Scripture—don't forget that the genealogy in Matthew and the genealogy in Luke give in one case that of Joseph and in the other case that of Mary; there are different names involved. But notice that verse 17 sums it all up: "So all the generations from Abraham to David are fourteen generations; and from David until the carrying away of Babylon are fourteen generations; and from the carrying away of Babylon unto Christ are fourteen generations."

These are crises in the history of the Jewish people, crises that pictured great times of hope but ended in failure and frustration. Abraham, through faith and obedience, was going to lead the people into the land, but he failed. Then there came David, who, through loyalty to God, was going to be the king of the people; but he too

failed, even the man after God's own heart. Then the result was Babylon, with its tragic bondage and captivity,
its disgrace and slavery. So, you see, it would seem that
the expectation of the Jews had simply come to an end.
There was no hope, for it all ended in slavery and corrup-
tion. The greatest human characters had failed, and the
result was captivity and bondage. It would seem as if
God's purposes had all been thwarted by human rebellion,
sin and unbelief.

Yet, somehow, they couldn't quite come to believe that
all hope was lost, and at a very critical hour of history the
prophet Isaiah spoke of this sign that God would give
them, of a virgin who would conceive; how, in some mys-
terious way, God was going to invade this little planet
Himself in the Person of His Son. Yet the centuries passed
by and the prophecy remained unfulfilled. The hope of
the Jewish people dwindled completely. In any event,
they had no faith to believe in a great Deliverer except
that it might be just a kind of escape from the tyranny of
an empire. But their hope had all gone.

You can never limit God's program to human ideas and
human conceptions. The idea of this people was that God
had come merely to make their lot a little bit more comfortable and save them from the consequences of their
rebellion and sin; that is all they thought a Deliverer
would mean. But God's program was far greater than
that. After all, what would be the use of dealing with the
consequences if He did not touch the cause? That would
be merely dealing with the fruit of the trouble instead of
really going to the root of it. It wasn't any use for God to
deal with the symptoms of sin unless, somehow, God
could strike at the very root of all the trouble. So Jesus
came, and I am afraid that many of us—in thinking of His

coming and of what He can do for us—have often thus limited God's program and plan for our own lives because of our limited conception of what He can do. We've asked Him to help us to deal with some of the symptoms of trouble in our hearts and in our experience, but we have never realized that God's program of redemption, power and liberation is so infinitely greater than anything we could ever ask Him to do for us. Jesus Christ did not come just to deal with a few symptoms of trouble in our hearts, to comfort and help us in one or two situations. No, He came to conduct a God-designed invasion that would go to the very root of the need.

I may be reaching someone who is not a believer in our Lord. If I were to ask you what you think Jesus Christ could do for you, you might say, "Well, perhaps He might help me a little bit to overcome problems, comfort me in times of trouble, and one day get me through to heaven." Have you ever really understood that God has come to do something drastic? This God-planned invasion which took place at Bethlehem was not just meant to touch the symptom; it was to go right down to the thing that brings us into slavery, and to strike at the root of it. I hope, therefore, that our anticipation of what Christ can do is not limited by our own feeble ideas.

As we look further, we see that Old Testament hope realized in this New Testament story, and what a beautiful story it is! It is so sacred and lovely. It would never have been known to us if Joseph and Mary had not told it. If you compare the account of the birth of our Lord in Matthew with the account given in Luke's Gospel, you notice immediately that there is a distinction. In Luke's Gospel it is given to us from the standpoint of Mary, her bewilderment and problems. But in Matthew's Gospel it is told from the standpoint of Joseph, his perplexity, his unbelief, his concern, his desire to protect this woman from scandal. His desire to do the right thing is told so simply and beautifully, and all his fears are suddenly removed when the angel of the Lord says: ". . . fear not, . . . that which is conceived in her is of the Holy Ghost" (v. 20); ". . . thou shalt call his name Jesus: for he shall save his people from their sins."

Some people seem to imagine that they don't need to believe in the virgin birth of our Lord to be Christian, that it is not really an essential part of the Christian faith. My friend, if you reject the virgin birth of Christ, you reject the deity of Christ. It is impossible to hold to one and not the other. The one who has come to show God to men, who has come to save us from our sins, must obviously be born into a human race and be part of it. That is the amazing condescension of God. It wasn't necessary, and God knows that is so. Justice would have been completely satisfied if the race had been wiped out; but God is love, and if that love is to be expressed, if men are to be saved, if the invasion from heaven is to strike at the root, then He must become part, not of a sinless humanity, but of a sinful, degraded, corrupt humanity. He must become one of them—a fact, indeed, I think we all can understand. But if He is to become one with us in order to save us from our sin, He must be free from the taint of sin which passes into all human life that is born after the will of the flesh. Somehow Jesus must come into this human race, be part of it and yet not of it, something it has never before produced by the normal method of birth. He must not be tainted with the sin of humanity. He has come to be like us in all things except our sin. You cannot explain the sinless life of our wonderful Lord unless you accept the truth of His miraculous birth.

This story, which is so simply and frankly told in the

Gospels, only confirms what Jesus said: "I am from above . . ."; "I am not of this world" (JOHN 8:23). And here is the answer of God to the hope of the people. What an amazing thing to think of our God, the eternal God, dwelling in the frail body of a little baby, taking upon Himself the nature (as I have said), not of a sinless race, but of a people who had rebelled against His rule, that He might not only save us from the consequences of rebellion but that He might break the power of it at its very source. That is the realization of the hope: ". . . he shall save his people from their sins."

When the angels said: ". . . thou shalt call his name Jesus," Joseph was not surprised at that, for there were lots of little boys called Jesus running about the streets; it was a very common name at that time. Today we give our children names and often we do not stop to think much about their meaning. We choose them because they are popular or attractive, or because they are family names. The name "Jesus" was not simply a popular name, because in those days names meant something. It had a tremendous significance. The Hebrew name for Jesus is "Joshua." Immediately my mind goes back to two Old Testament characters: the one, a great commander-in-chief who led the people into tremendous battles, through the wilderness into the land, but could not give them rest; the other Joshua was a priest, living in the days of Zechariah, who stood in filthy garments before the Lord, and could not remove the stain of sin from the people or from himself as he ministered.

The Hebrew "Joshua" is really two words. There were only two men who got out of Egypt and into Canaan; the rest perished because of unbelief. One was called Caleb, and the other was Joshua. But Joshua was not always called by that name. His name when he was a younger man was Hosea (meaning "saviour"), but one day Moses changed his name and called him Joshua, and that name is really a combination of two Jewish names, "Hosea" and "Jehovah"—"Saviour-God." *Thou shalt call His name Joshua, Jesus, Saviour-God.*

The two things that the Old Testament Joshuas could not do, Jesus came to do. Joshua led the people into battle, conflict and victory, but he could not lead them into rest. The Old Testament priest could not lead the people into cleansing and deliverance. There is a connection here: no rest because no cleansing; the captain was helpless to lead them into rest because they were unclean. The Old Testament priest was unable to lead them into cleansing for he had no power to do it of himself—he himself was unclean.

". . . thou shalt call his name Jesus: for he shall save his people from their sins." And what does He do when He saves His people from their sins? Praise the Lord, He takes them out of bondage, through a wilderness, into battle and victory, and then into rest! "There remaineth therefore a rest to the people of God" (HEBREWS 4:9). How does this great Jesus of ours lead us into rest? Praise the Lord, He has offered Himself for us to give us cleansing! There is no rest in your life if it is unclean. He can cleanse you and give you rest. Oh, how much greater is the realization than the Old Testament hope! I think it is so thrilling and wonderful to know that Jesus can give you those two things that you need today more than anything else in the world—cleansing and rest.

At Jesus' birth, when Joseph gave Him the name, it was only a prophecy. Go on another generation and read the Apostle Paul: Jesus, "being in the form of God, counted it not a thing to be grasped at to be counted equal with God; but emptied himself and took upon himself the form of a servant and was made in the likeness of men." That is Paul's story of the incarnation. But to continue: ". . . he humbled himself, and became obedient unto death, even the death of the cross. Wherefore God also hath highly exalted him, and given him a name which is above every name" (PHILIPPIANS 2:6-10). And what is that name?

Joseph called Him Jesus because the angel told him to, and that was a prophecy that He would save His people from their sins. One day, on the cross outside Jerusalem, the prophecy became a fact. The work was finished, the blood was shed, the sacrifice was over, and there was a way through for the guiltiest and foulest of souls into the presence of God by the cleansing of His blood. It became a fact, and on the day when He ascended into heaven and sat down at the right hand of God, it became a flaming evangel that swept through the world for two thousand years, because at the name of Jesus every knee shall bow. I should say they will! He is the only One who can bring men that which they desperately need: cleansing and rest. Therefore, before Him every other must recede, and before Him every knee shall bow. When He was born as a little Babe in a manger, that name declared why He had come; that was His purpose. When He rose triumphant over the grave and God gave Him that name in glory, it declared that God's purpose had been accomplished and that the victory had been won.

Abraham and David failed. Abraham failed because of lack of faith and obedience. Jesus triumphed by faith and obedience. David failed because of lack of loyalty to the Lord. Jesus triumphed because He delighted to do the will of God. There is the Old Testament anticipation, so small; and there is the New Testament realization, so tremendous, so glorious and so wonderful.

Read it again; Emmanuel, "God with us." Jesus—Saviour-God—cleansing and giving rest. As we look back over the centuries and remember that God became a Baby, was born of a virgin in human life, I would ask you very earnestly, Has God been born in you? Are cleansing and rest something that your heart has answered as I have been talking to you, saying, "That is what I need, but I haven't got it. Of course, I want Jesus, because then He would make my lot a little more comfortable. It would be nice to be a Christian and to know that one day I would get to heaven, and I think it is right that I should know something about this Christmas message and what it means"? But in spite of all this, do the two greatest needs in your life remain unsatisfied? "He came unto his own, and his own received him not. But as many as received him, to them gave he power to become the sons of God, even to them that believe on his name: Which were born, not of blood, nor of the will of the flesh, nor of the will of man, but of God" (JOHN 1:11-13). Jesus came to save by a miracle of birth; He will save you by another miracle of the new birth. It is not by blood (not by your natural heritage, no matter how high in the social scale any may be), nor by the will of the flesh (not by your natural desire or personal effort), nor by the will of man (not by the intervention of any other, not in a way that anybody in any church can do for you), but of God.

He came to save, He was born miraculously, and His purpose of rest and cleansing is fulfilled in your life when you are born miraculously by the same Holy Spirit who brought Jesus to be a Baby in the womb of the virgin Mary. By the same Spirit He becomes incarnate in your life, and from that day on, praise the Lord, you enter into rest and into cleansing!

I hope something of the fire, the wonder, the glow of the coming of a little Babe to bring us rest and cleansing will grip your soul even today, for you see, If God be with us—and He is—well, then what? Sorrow, perhaps, but it will never overwhelm us. Temptation, yes, but it will never conquer if we are trusting in Him. Suffering, yes, but He will never allow us to be tested beyond that we are able. Death, certainly, unless He comes first, but there is no sting in it. Therefore, if God be for us, the word "impossible" is out of our vocabulary for ever. There is no such thing in the will of God as impossibilities, if God be with us—our Emmanuel.

5

THE REALITY OF DEMON-POSSESSION

. . . when he was come out of the ship, immediately there met him out of the tombs a man with an unclean spirit. . . . And they come to Jesus, and see him that was possessed with the devil, and had the legion, sitting, and clothed, and in his right mind: and they were afraid—MARK 5:2, 15

Those two verses fling a boundary around one of the many instances in the New Testament in which our Lord encountered men possessed by evil spirits; and we must beware of imagining that we are facing in this story something that is exceptional, or something that happened long ago, as though the adversaries and conditions related here do not exist today. As a matter of fact, we are considering this subject at a time when we are moving rapidly toward the climax of this age, to the day when Jesus Christ Himself shall come and His Kingdom shall be established.

All along the journey we are surrounded and beset by evil hosts of every possible kind. The way they express themselves may vary, but their deadly activity is more rampant, more powerful, more poisonous, more foul, more deadly than ever; and this, of course, is exactly what our Lord said would happen on the very eve of His return. Now this is a great challenge to us, and it is also a great comfort, for it is perfectly clear that in the Lord Jesus Christ, and in Him alone, there is the force of authority over all this evil power.

Before we come to grips with this particular passage, I would like to consider what the Bible has to say about demon-possession. The Gospel of Mark gives a great deal of space to this incident and, indeed, I would say that Mark's Gospel has as its major emphasis the fact of the dreadful experience of human beings in the grip of demons. To trace this quickly through the Gospel, in Chapter 1:23-27 is recorded our Lord's first encounter with a man with an unclean spirit in the synagogue. Please notice that as soon as the unclean spirit encountered Christ, it cried out, saying, "Let us alone; what have we to do with thee, thou Jesus of Nazareth?" There follows the record of our Lord dealing in authority with the powers of darkness.

You have the same thing in verses 32-34 of the same chapter: ". . . at even, when the sun did set, they brought unto him all that were diseased, and them that were possessed with devils." ". . . he preached in their synagogues throughout all Galilee, and cast out devils" (v. 39). Again, in Chapter 3:11, 12, you read this: ". . . unclean spirits, when they saw him, fell down before him, and cried, saying, Thou art the Son of God. And he straitly charged them that they should not make him known."

You will observe that in verse 15 of the same chapter, Jesus, in sending His disciples out before Him, gave them power over unclean spirits and to cast out demons. Also, in verses 22-30, is recorded the Lord's rebuke to the scribes who accused Him of casting out demons by the power of Beelzebub, the prince of demons; and His stern rebuke and warning that while every sin could be forgiven, there was one sin which would never be forgiven, and this was attributing to the devil the work of the Holy Spirit. Moving beyond the incident which we are soon to consider, in Chapter 6:7 we find Him sending out the disciples two by two and giving them power over unclean spirits. In Chapter 7:25-30 is the incident of the Syrophoenician woman who had a young daughter with an unclean spirit. Immediately following the events on the Mount of Transfiguration, our Lord descended into the valley and met a man whose son was possessed by an evil spirit (9:17-27). You will recall, in Chapter 16:7-9, the story of the Lord's resurrection appearance, that "he appeared first to Mary Magdalene, out of whom He had cast seven devils"; and in verse 17 the risen Christ sent out all His disciples with power to cast out demon spirits.

Here, then, is the major emphasis of Mark's whole Gospel. This is something you cannot ignore. It is right at the very heart of the message of the Christian faith. Now, of course, I know that some people suggest that Christ was using the language of His age, and that these people were not really demon-possessed at all. That would mean He was taking the side of superstition, and we could never accept that suggestion. Other writers and theologians suggest this is merely the language of the writers of the Gospels, trying to explain something that Jesus did; that He never talked with demons, that He merely produced a kind of quietness in the minds and attitudes of people, and this is the way the disciples interpreted it. If you go on that road, you immediately destroy all the authority of the New Testament.

I believe that this is a subject we have to face realistically in the light of all that the Word of God has to say about it. May I underline this point: in the *Revised Version*, in the 1901 edition, the translators always observe a distinction between the devil and demons. The word "devil" is the one word that is used of the one, strange, powerful, spiritual personality called "Satan," which word means "adversary"; the word "demon" is always used in relation to the evil or unclean spirit which inhabits human beings. The scribes charged the Lord with casting out

demons by Beelzebub, the prince of demons (MARK 3:22).
In other words, they recognized the principle that there
were a host of evil spirits who had a leader. Christ, of
course, denied their accusation, but not their concept of
evil spirits. Indeed, His whole argument was based upon
their accuracy when He said: "If Satan cast out Satan,
then his kingdom is divided and cannot stand." Our Lord
admits the fact that there is an underworld of evil, foul,
spiritual beings who are controlled, ordered, governed,
and at the disposal of this one master-satanic personality,
Satan himself.

We might ask ourselves, Who are these strange, spiritual, evil forces? Nothing can be dogmatically said about
them, but the New Testament makes it perfectly plain
that they were always seeking some material resting
place. They could not exist except within human personality or some kind of physical being, and they were always
hankering after something or someone through whom
they could express their foul, devilish ways. The generally
accepted view (into which I have no time to go, but
which I believe is an accurate one, substantiated from the
Word of God) is that these evil spirits, long before the fall
of man described in Genesis, were led in revolt against the
authority of God by their leader, Satan himself, Lucifer,
the son of the morning. Reference is to be found to this in
Isaiah 14 and Revelation 12, where we are told that no
less than one third of the whole host of heaven were involved in the revolt which Satan carried out in his attempt to usurp the authority of the throne of all the universe, and for that was cast into hell. I believe that we
have Scriptural authority for this suggestion. Certainly
the New Testament clearly reveals the existence of these
beings, their access to human people—always, please

note, with a view to creating havoc and destruction and ruin. You will find no instance in the whole of the Bible of a good spirit possessing anybody, except it be the Holy Spirit of God.

These are some of the things that are taught in the Word of God concerning this whole matter of demon-possession. But I want you to see them operating in the incident which is described for us in Mark 5. This is a terrifying subject, but a very wonderful one; I believe that it is one of the most common, most dangerous, and most unrecognized factors of this modern world situation, which more often than not is being tackled completely superficially by the psychiatrist who is not a Christian. (Let me be perfectly clear about this. I believe that a Christian psychiatrist has a great ministry, and it is my privilege constantly to cooperate and have fellowship with such; but I believe that a psychiatrist who is not a Christian could be a great menace to humanity.)

What, then, was the condition of this poor man? Let us look at him: he was "a man with an unclean spirit" (v.2). The terrifying thing about this is that the literal translation of this word would be "a man *in* an unclean spirit." In other words, when you met him, you were much more impressed with the unclean spirit than with the man. He was it. Just as the Christian would claim that his life is "hid with Christ in God"; just as when you meet a genuine, born-again believer filled with the Holy Ghost, Holy-Spirit-possessed, you become conscious most of all, not of the man, but of the Lord. So in the life of this man, his personality was completely buried, and he was absolutely involved from the crown of his head to the sole of his foot with the evil spirit. The *Revised Version* puts it: ". . . a man possessed with, or possessed by, an evil spirit."

There are a few up-to-date words which describe this man's condition from this portion of Scripture. First, a condition of isolation, verse 3: he "had his dwelling among the tombs"—as far away from society as he could get.

Second, a condition of lawlessness, verse 3: ". . . no man could bind him, no, not with chains: because that he has been often bound with fetters and chains, and the chains had been plucked asunder by him, and the fetters broken in pieces: neither could any man tame him." This man broke through every restraint that was put upon him. Nothing could hold him—he just snapped his bonds in pieces.

Third, a condition of restlessness, verse 5: ". . . . always, night and day, he was in the mountains, and in the tombs, crying. . . ."

Fourth, a condition of self-inflicted suffering, verse 5: ". . . cutting himself with stones."

My final word would be that he was a danger to society, for Matthew tells us (though Mark does not record this in exactly the same words): ". . . he was . . . exceeding fierce, so that no man might pass that way" (8:28).

The picture that is in my mind is terrifying. What a hideous picture of the effect upon a man when he is possessed by an unclean spirit! What a revelation of the impotence of everything apart from the power of Jesus Christ to tame him, to save him, to set him free! Review these words again: *isolation, lawlessness, restlessness, suffering, a danger to other people.* Is that out of date? Is that so far removed from us today? Are not the symptoms of this thing everywhere? Is that not the condition of multitudes of people in the world right now? This is vivid, twentieth-century demon-possession. But it is nearer than

Skid Row. It may be as near as someone reading this today.

Notice not only the condition of the man, but also the character of the demons. I think that the most significant aspect of the whole incident was the attitude of the demons when they met Jesus Christ. This is true not only in this instance, but of every instance when He encountered them. ". . . when he saw Jesus afar off, he ran and worshipped him" (v. 6)—an attitude of submission. Notice his question in verse 7: "What have I to with thee?" or, putting it literally, "What have we in common, Jesus, Thou Son of the Most High God?"

I must point out some things in passing that I do not want you to miss. The devil is a good enough theologian to acknowledge the deity of Jesus Christ, and if you recall for a moment those who did—demons, angels, men, friends and foes alike, all who acknowledged His deity— we might ask ourselves, what right has a Unitarian to be called Christian?

Observe the language of these unclean spirits, as a legion of them spoke through this man (v. 7): "I adjure thee"—which means "I beg you." Verse 10: ". . . he besought him. . . ." Verse 12: they "besought him . . ." that if indeed they were to be driven out of the man they might enter into the swine, revealing their desire for some material influence to satisfy the strange, hellish appetite of their nature.

I would press this home to you again, that you see the picture here. The legion of demons had so possessed the man that he was almost unrecognizable. His personality was shrunk as they held him in their power. He was absolutely impotent and helpless, crushed. The poor wretch! But there came a moment when demons and all met Jesus

Christ and they began to cringe. I see the picture here of a man helpless, desolate, lonely, desperate, tortured, and yet in the presence of Jesus he begins to yearn for deliverance, but he is unwilling to be set free. He bows in adoration and in prayer, but he is defiant and fearful the next moment. With one breath he is longing for liberty, with the next he is clinging to his past. At one moment he pleads to be set free, at the next moment he holds to the thing that grips him.

Is this far away, or is it desperately, terrifyingly near? In your life, do you know anything about two voices, two forces within you? Do you know anything of a love of evil, and yet a longing for good? In other words, do you know something about Dr. Jekyll and Mr. Hyde?

There is a tremendously solemn word in verse 15, where the story concludes by telling us that the man was "in his right mind." He had been driven absolutely mad by the spiritual battle in his own soul. May I venture to say that insanity is far more often connected with spiritual demons than we recognize. What about our mental institutions today? They are overcrowded, and I humbly suggest to you that the reason why the vast majority of people are there is that they have been driven out of their minds by the rush of evil at one moment and the next moment a longing for good, and no answer to the problem. Now, of course, may I respectfully say that the psychiatrist who is not a Christian will play down that situation. He will say that sin is merely an unfortunate reflex which can be cured by medical process, or something of this kind. He will play down the root and deal with the mind; he will go back into infancy and trace back into individual records to see how this situation has built up. In the name of heaven, I can tell him how it has built up! It has built up because that poor soul has lived for years.

fighting a battle with sin and self and evil and a depraved mind, longing for deliverance, but nobody has got along-side to tell him that Jesus saves.

You see this whole business on an international level. You see it in dictators and godless rulers. These men are unchecked by any moral standards. They don't know any law except the laws they create and break. How futile are all the pacts and all the attempts to reconcile that situation! Such men don't live on that level. You see this in family life, where love is no more than physical appetite and passion, where tempers get out of control, where harsh tongues are unchecked. You see it in personal life, where a man or a woman is governed by a whole legion of evil inside.

Do not think of a minister above that which he ought to be thought about: but for the mighty power of the in-dwelling Jesus in my heart, my life would be a play-ground for hell every day. I can look back over years when I didn't know the answer to this, and many times I attempted to put on the chains of self-discipline and self-effort, and so-called moral rearmament. But I put them on in vain. Before long an unclean spirit would snap them asunder. The flash of temper, the passionate outburst, the uncontrolled spirit—all were the outcome, not of some mental derangement, but of satanic power in my heart. I tell you, this is terrifying indeed. Oh, but there is the song of a soul set free in my heart. How I love that hymn of Charles Wesley's:

> Jesus, the name high over all,
> In Hell, or earth or sky;
> Angels and men before Him fall,
> And devils fear and fly.

Jesus, the name to sinners dear,
The name to sinners given;
He scatters all their guilty fear;
And turns their Hell to Heaven.

Jesus the prisoner's fetters breaks,
And bruises Satan's head;
Power into strengthless souls He speaks,
And life into the dead.

Finally, I would point you to the conquering Christ. He spoke one word, and I think He spoke it quietly: "Come out of the man, thou unclean spirit" (v. 8). Oh, I wish I could have been there and seen it happen! One quiet word from the Master before whom already the powers of hell had cringed in fear! One word was enough!

Notice that Jesus did not begin by clothing the man, but by saving him. The only way to get a man out of the slum is to get the slum out of the man. Social reform is very good, but the only hope for the human heart is not changed circumstances, but a new nature. See how Jesus talked to him; He asked him, "What is your name?" And I believe He was just probing through all the unclean spirits in this poor, wretched soul, and calling tenderly, lovingly, affectionately, "What is your name?" He was calling him to a sense of his personality, to what God intended him to be. Notice the answer—what a struggle was going on? "My name is Legion: for we are many" (v. 9). My name—then the devil shuts him up. A man who for a moment was almost free was held in the grip of the unclean spirit. Then with one word of authority that you have in Matthew 8:32 (in Mark 5:13 Jesus gave them leave to go out), the Lord chased them all and said, "Go."

They asked for another lodging place; they knew they were being put out, and that they had met their Master, so they said, "O Thou Son of God, if we must be put out of this man, send us into the swine." I'm fully aware of the problems about that. You may have read what Huxley has to say, and others, but I don't care what they have to say about it. This story is not told to inform us about the destruction of one thousand pigs for the salvation of one soul. It has been told to remind us that in that command Jesus was rebuking the traffic of the Jew with forbidden goods.

What is the conclusion of this? In verse 17 the crowd prayed Jesus to depart. In other words, they preferred the swine to the Saviour. They were much more concerned about their material loss than the salvation of a soul. Here is a mystery. Let your spiritual ears be wide open! Let the Holy Spirit plant a seed never to die in your hearts! May it sound the word of warning in your soul! Jesus commands devils; He only pleads with you. The prayer of the people who wanted Him to go was answered. I think of the authority of Jesus Christ as He faced that demon-possessed man and spoke with such absolute finality to all the demons as He said, "Go." Then I think of Him turning His back upon that country and district, walking away from them, and answering their prayers to depart. There was as much authority in the back that turned away as in the face that said, "Go."

It is a dreadful thing to tell Jesus to depart. In preferring sin to salvation, that is exactly what you are doing—listening to the one voice that wants to retain that which has held you in its grip, instead of listening to the voice of Jesus who says, "Come, Take My yoke upon you and learn of Me, and you shall find rest instead of restlessness." You can bid Jesus depart this moment. In the words of Mat-

thew 7:21: "Not every one that says unto me, Lord, Lord,
shall enter into the kingdom of heaven; but he that doeth
the will of my Father which is in heaven. Many will say to
me in that day, Lord, Lord, have we not prophesied in thy
name? and in thy name cast out devils. . . ? then will I
profess unto them, I never knew you." Let it be said with
solemnity, with love, with conviction from heaven, that
when a man says to Jesus, "Depart," one day Jesus is
going to say exactly the same to that man.

What about this man? As we conclude with a picture of
him here, we find him sitting at the feet of Jesus, clothed
and in his right mind. The storm is over, the isolation is
ended, the resting is in his heart, the chains have fallen off
and there is peace. He prays also that he might be with
Him, but Jesus didn't answer that prayer: "Jesus suffered
him not, but saith unto him, Go home to thy friends, and
tell them how great things the Lord hath done for thee,
and hath had compassion on thee" (v. 19).

It is one of the biggest mistakes of our day to hawk
around a new convert to as many meetings as possible to
display the story of his conversion instead of sending him
home to tell and live the changed life right there. There
are some movements today that are doing more harm than
good. Oh, but that restored man wasn't sent from Christ,
nor are you! He was sent *for* Christ, back to his home. I
have often pictured that homecoming in my mind and
wondered what it was like. Would there be some little
children playing outside the house, and a wife perhaps
doing the washing inside? Suddenly from outside the door
there is a scream of terror, "Mummy, help! Daddy's
back!" and the children fly into the arms of their mother.
Is their father going to harm them? The mother is terri-
fied, too. The door opens and she hasn't to do more than

look in her husband's face before she sees she has a new husband!

All the hounds of hell inhabiting that man knew that Jesus was Lord. Do you know it? However desperate the condition of a soul may be, there is close at hand a mighty Saviour. He is more powerful than a whole legion of devils. Do you believe it? Then what must you do? Claim it. Don't cry one moment for His deliverance, and the next moment hate it. Cease listening to one voice one minute and the next to the other, sinking under the control of the legion that possesses you. Let Him hear you say, "My name is. . . ." Lift your heart to Him and bid all the powers of darkness retreat, and by faith step to the throne of God, in the name of Jesus, and say, "Thank You, Lord. Your blood was shed to deliver me from this." Claim the victory that His blood and risen life secured for you.

6

THE DIVINE PATTERN OF
DELIVERANCE FOR THE CHRISTIAN

> *. . . it shall come to pass in that day, that I will
> seek to destroy all the nations that come against
> Jersusalem. And I will pour upon . . . the inhabi-
> tants of Jerusalem, the spirit of grace and of
> supplications: and they shall look upon me whom
> they have pierced, and they shall mourn for him*
> —ZECHARIAH 12:9, 10

There is, of course, a literal fulfillment of these words
which is evidently in the future. There is a time coming
when the Jews as a nation will recognize Jesus Christ as
their Messiah. You will recall the scene (in the Book of
Genesis) in Joseph's palace where he made himself known
to his brethren and they looked on him whom they had
cast into a pit, and they mourned with bitter tears. That
scene will be literally enacted before the eyes of the
whole world one day. In the second verse of this chapter,
Zechariah tells us, as the messenger of the Lord, that this
recognition of Christ as the Messiah of the Jews and the
reconciliation of the whole nation to Him is going to take
place when their enemies will be besieging Jerusalem,
when the city is surrounded by its foes.

The teaching of Scripture is clear; look at just one example in Ezekiel 36:24-26: "I will take you from among
the heathen, and gather you out of all countries, and will
bring you into your own land. Then will I sprinkle clean
water upon you, and ye shall be clean: from all your filthiness, and from all your idols, will I cleanse you. A new
heart also will I give you, and a new spirit will I put

within you." The Jews will return to their own land in unbelief, but they will recognize the Lord Jesus as their Messiah when He comes again to deliver them. You and I live in an amazing generation when very much of this has taken place before our eyes, and when for the first time since A.D. 70 there is now a national state of Israel.

The Jew is returning rapidly to his own land in unbelief. The first chapter of Revelation, verse 7, says: "Behold, he cometh with clouds; and every eye shall see him, and they also which pierced him: and all kindreds of the earth shall wail because of him." Zechariah tells us that this is going to happen in a day of *assault* when the whole city is to be surrounded by its enemies.

But this day of assault is also a day of *deliverance*, for verse 9 of this chapter tells us that the Lord will destroy every enemy that will come against His people. And this day of deliverance is such because it is a day of *prayer*, for verse 10 tells us that in that day the Lord will pour upon His people the Spirit of grace and supplication. And furthermore, it is to be a day of *recognition* when they shall look upon Him whom they have pierced, their crucified Lord.

Now, if we turn to this prophetic chapter in the light of the revelation of the New Testament, it takes on a meaning which has a tremendous significance for your life and mine. As a matter of fact, it touches the depths of Christian experience. It points us along the way to the richest Holy Ghost blessing that we can have this side of heaven, and it is from this practical aspect I desire to consider it. The New Testament distinguishes between the earthly and the heavenly Jerusalem. You remember that the writer to the Hebrews says, ". . . ye are come unto mount Sion, and unto the city of the living God, the heavenly

Jerusalem, and to an innumerable company of angels, to the general assembly and church of the firstborn, which are written in heaven, and to God the Judge of all, and to the spirits of just men made perfect, and to Jesus the mediator of the new covenant, and to the blood of sprinkling, that speaketh better things than that of Abel" (12: 22-24). Yes, God's people have come there now, and because of this we sing:

> Saviour, if of Zion's city
>   I through grace a member am,
> Let the world deride or pity,
>   I will glory in Thy name.

We have come to the heavenly Jerusalem, to Jesus, to the blood of sprinkling. And because we have come there, this, for God's people, is a day of assault, a day when the church is surrounded by every enemy imaginable. But in the purpose of God the day of assault is to be a day of deliverance. God is ready to do something for His people, to deliver them in every assault, no matter how tremendous or overpowering it may be. God's purpose for His people in every situation is always, all the time, victory through Jesus' name. But God does not work for His people until first of all He has worked in them. It is only when He has done something in us privately, personally, intimately, that He is able to do something for us publicly for the glory of His name. The day of assault is to be a day of deliverance.

But it is only a day of deliverance because first of all it has become a day of prayer and supplication, which has in itself made it to be a day of recognition, which has brought us to a day of mourning. I want you to look at these things closely, for you see, when the burden of prayer comes upon God's people there comes to us a new recognition of Jesus, the One whom we have pierced; and for Him our hearts are broken, and then we bless His name, in the day of deliverance. We can never play with the divine pattern or reverse the divine order or short-cut the way of heaven's blessing.

It is interesting that this chapter in Zechariah begins by telling us that this is the burden of the Lord for His people. ". . . the Lord," says the Scripture, "which stretcheth forth the heavens, and layeth the foundation of the earth. . . ." This is our God, this is our Jesus, this is the One in whose presence we meet, this is the God of battles and the God of victory, for not only is He the One who "stretcheth forth the heavens, and layeth the foundation of the earth"; this is the One, says the Scripture, who "formeth the spirit of man within him." In this message, therefore, is the burden of the Lord for your life and mine today.

A DAY OF ASSAULT

This is a day of assault (v. 2): ". . . they shall be in the siege . . . against Jerusalem." Ever since the church was born at Pentecost, it has been living in a state of siege. It has always lived in a hostile world; it has never known anything but tribulation when it has been true to its calling. The Christian is always being attacked, and Paul warns us, in the Epistle to the Ephesians, to put on "all the armour of God," that we might put out the incendiary bombs of the devil. That warfare has never ceased. From time to time—in such times, for instance, as the Second World War—it has assumed an appearance of anarchy and gigantic proportions. In other times—such as this in which we live today—it has assumed an intensity the like of which, I sincerely believe, has never been known in history. The greatest discomfiture in hell is always caused by the life of the child of God who is true to his witness. All the enemy's fire is trained upon such a man, for the testimony of such a Christian is a witness to the power of the blood of Jesus; this man, therefore, is inevitably surrounded by enemies who do their utmost to stamp out resistance, kill his testimony, silence his lips and freeze up his heart until the man, to all intents and purposes, is spiritually a nonentity.

You and I live in a day of siege. I think I would carry most, if not all, of you with me when I say that having been a Christian for some thirty years now, I have never been so conscious of the siege of the enemy as I am in these days. Are you not conscious of his ceaseless efforts to trip you up and deaden your Christian experience? Must you not consciously and constantly admit that time and again he has taken you by surprise, off your guard? Does he not sometimes seem to throttle you? You have only been born again perhaps a few weeks, and have become discouraged to discover that the spiritual warfare is far more intense now than at the moment when you were converted. You have only to look at your newspaper every day to know that hell is literally let loose on earth at this time, and every true Christian knows what it is to be constantly besieged. When a Christian falls under the attacks of the enemy, and when there are casualties in the battle, as there inevitably are, let us not condemn; let us rather remember that the man or woman who has fallen probably put up a desperate fight before he or she went down. Yes, this is a day of intense assault upon the church.

A DAY OF DELIVERANCE

But then, an assault of the devil is never an excuse for the Christian to go down. And in verse 9 it is made perfectly clear to us that the day of assault is to be a day of deliverance. "The burden of the Lord"—and that tremendous phrase simply means that which lies heavy on the heart of God for His people—the very burden upon the heart of God for His people is to make this day of assault into a day of total victory, when there shall be the triumph of the people of God over all the assault of hell. The intensity of the assault, I repeat, is no excuse for our failure. It is no excuse for our giving in; it is no excuse for quitting, no excuse for throwing our hands up and saying, "It is not worth it." The promise of this Word is that though all the power of the aggressor be gathered together against Jerusalem, yet He will destroy its every foe.

I remind you that this deliverance is not something which comes from heaven automatically. It is not something that God guarantees will be inevitable in the life of His people, for He never accomplishes any warfare, any victory in the heart of any one of us, independent of ourselves. First of all, before God will step in to deliver His church, before your own Christian life will ring with the joy of victory in your soul, before in public everybody will bear witness to the amazing transformation of your life, first of all God must do something *in* you. He will make something of you. Look at verse 2: "I will make Jerusalem a cup of trembling unto all people." Verse 3: "I will make Jerusalem a burdensome stone for all people." Verse 6: "I will make the governors of Judah like . . . a torch of fire in a sheaf." In other words, putting it into simple, everyday language, the power of Jerusalem—the people of God—will be such that it will make the enemy reel and retreat in disorder! Jerusalem shall cut the enemy to pieces! Jerusalem shall be like a flame which burns up the foe!

This is the divine pattern for the overcoming of every assault of the devil upon your soul. Your life and mine should make all hell tremble! Your life should be as impregnable, as unshakable as a rock against any foes which may dash themselves against it, only to dash themselves to pieces! Your life should be like a flame, a burning flame, which burns out the dross of self and love of sin in you and burns in the beauty of the Lord your God. The day of assault is to be the day of deliverance.

Do you remember that it was said of John the Baptist that he was a burning and a shining light? He shone because he burned, because a flame burned within him; therefore his life shone. We long to shine! Yes, but God will not make us shine till we have learned to burn. That is what God wants to do with us. And how many times we have cried to God to do it. But you see, He can only do that for us if first of all He does something *in* us.

A DAY OF PRAYER

Let us take a step farther. The day of assault, of which you and I are only too conscious, is to be a day of wonderful deliverance when the enemy trembles against us and retreats in disorder. But it is only this because it has been a day of prayer. "I will pour . . . upon the inhabitants of Jerusalem the spirit of grace and of supplications." Man's way of resisting an assault like this (which is too often our way) is to rise up and attempt to retaliate. God's way is to drive His people to their knees, and this is something that only God can do. There is so much spiritual pride in all of us that when we are conscious of the day of siege, almost the last thing we think about is that the only answer is to be upon our face before God for the power that He alone can give to resist the enemy. We determine to resist, and He drives us to prayer.

How desperately we need to seek Him for this today! How we need to ask Him to forgive us for the coldness of our praying! How we need to ask Him for a Spirit of prayer that would really put the prayer meeting of the church right in the very front of our program! This is our greatest lack: the Spirit of supplication. We lament the barrenness of our service, we deplore the lack of evidence of spiritual power; and yet how little of our time is really given to earnest waiting upon God in the Spirit of prayer and supplication. I believe that this gift has departed from the church at this time. I believe the church is bereft without it. Some spend time waiting and praying that God would give the gift of tongues, and we have not even learned to pray in one tongue. We have not learned the first lesson of the child of God to cry to his Father for the touch of the Holy Ghost authority. I know that public prayer is by no means everything, but I do know that the praying church is the victorious church, and the prayer-less church is the defeated church. How many of us who share the service of the church really share the burden of it in prayer?

A few years ago in Chicago, during the Billy Graham Crusade, we saw some tremendous things happen. The fruit of it all is beginning to emerge—the evidence of the working of the Spirit, the evidence of a true work of grace in hundreds of lives. Of course, there was chaff among wheat; but there certainly was wheat! It all took place because a man stood up, clothed with the authority of the Holy Ghost, anointed with power, yes, and spoke as "Thus saith the Lord!" And with that mighty authority there came conviction, blessing and conversion. I can truly say I do not envy Billy Graham his gift. God has given to him a unique and wonderful gift of evangelism. But I do envy his prayer support. I suppose he is the most prayed-for Christian in the world, certainly in the United States.

When I come to my pulpit on a Sunday morning, how many have met for prayer beforehand? Remember that a prayerless pew means a powerless pulpit. The prayer meeting ought to be the largest meeting of the week. How I covet such a fellowship. If there is anything we urgently need at this hour, that is it. There will never be a deliverance for any church until that church is on its face, pleading with God for the blessing.

A DAY OF RECOGNITION

What happens when we pray is that the day of prayer becomes a day of recognition. Says the Scripture, ". . . they shall look upon me whom they have pierced" (v. 10). Prayer brings recognition. Prayer brings the sense of conviction. Prayer tells me that my wretched pride and my selfishness and my sin and my rebellion against God— all of this—have crucified my Lord, and thrust a spear into His side. Prayer breaks my heart. Prayer brings Calvary right before my face, and that leads to victory. And what do you think victory is? What do you think deliverance is? A great shout and a great noise and a great triumphal procession? Oh, no! Let me tell you what victory is.

When you are forgotten or neglected or set at naught and you smile inwardly, glorying in the insult, this is victory. When your good is evil spoken of, when your wishes are crossed and your taste offended and your advice ignored, your opinion ridiculed and you take it in patient, loving silence, this is victory. When you are content with any food, any raiment, any climate, any society, any solitude, any interruption, this is victory. When you bear with any disorder, any irregularity, and any unpunctuality and any annoyance, this is victory. When you stand face to face with folly, waste, extravagance, spiritual insensibility of other people and endure it all as Jesus endured it, this is victory. When you never care to record your own good works or talk about the blessing God has given you or to itch after praise of men and you can love to be truly unknown, this is victory.

The day of prayer and supplication is a day of recognition when I see Jesus again and I see how defeated I have been. On my face before God, this leads *to the day of mourning.* ". . . they shall mourn for him. . . ." Not for themselves, not in self-pity, not in the things that have happened to us, but they shall mourn *for Him.*

Deliverance in the day of assault is not by lifting us up, but it is by breaking us down. For the broken heart is the heart that God makes into a flame. There He burns like a flame, and therefore the church is irresistible in its power and authority because it has been in prayer and supplication to Calvary and it has seen the sin of prayerlessness which has resulted in all the area of defeat.

Oh! that God today might speak to our hearts through His Word and remind us again and again of this tremendous promise that in that day when all of His people are attacked, as they have never been attacked before, His purpose in this situation—not simply in a future prophetic day, but now, in His church—is that of absolute victory through the power of the name of Jesus. And all of that is for you and me in our battle today where you and I are living now. But it is only for us when God has brought us by His Spirit into His presence, and we have seen Jesus again and have mourned for Him, and our hearts have been broken. May He lead us in the way of victory and deliverance this day and all other days, till Jesus comes.

7

THE SANCTITY OF MARRIAGE

EPHESIANS 5:22-33

The Bible speaks to our times. Yes! And never more clearly, or authoritatively, or with such solemn warning as when it speaks about the subject of marriage and the home.

The Christian faith, rightly applied, has immense social implications, and the application of its principles to the home is the most important and urgent need of today. The Christian home is the most sacred institution on earth, and the perfecting of it is the masterpiece of the gospel in its impact upon society. There is nothing so wonderful in all the world as a perfectly united home, and it takes the power of Christ and the grace of His Spirit in order to produce the full glory of it. When it is seen thus, its loveliness is diffused all around. For a Christian home is the example of unselfishness, sacrificial love and loyalty. Those who learn those qualities at home inevitably must be the means of spreading them wherever they go.

The home where Jesus is Lord is like a watered garden —like a spring whose waters fail not and make glad all who so sorely need its graciousness. I would dare to say that the vast majority of the troubles of our day owe their origin to the collapse of this divine institution, and the tragic and devastating inroads which prevalent customs have made upon it. It has been assailed with terrible subtlety from every side. The stress of life, the employment of women in industry, the severity of competition in business and in school, the craze for pleasure, the invasion within the very doors of home of television with, too often, its disgusting and revolting attack upon sex and the sanctity of marriage—all of these have loudly and rudely thrust open the door of "home," a word once so dear to all men, until now it is scarcely recognizable for what it used to be, and from it has gone the mark of divine sacredness. A veritable onslaught has been made on the source of this country's strength, and it cannot but have disastrous consequences.

It is, therefore, no wonder that the closing paragraphs of an epistle like that to the Ephesians is devoted in so large measure to domestic life. One might think at first glance that this was rather an anticlimax. The first three chapters have been occupied with the most wonderful truths of redemption: the eternal purpose of God, the election of His people, the atonement of Christ and the concern that we might be filled with all the fullness of God.

Surely some tremendous and almost blinding gaze into future glory will be the only fitting climax to such teaching! Instead we find ourselves as an intimate family circle within the doors of a home. The home is for a moment everything—as much as if all hope and duty were centered there, and all the great blessings of God in Christ were to see their most precious fulfillment there.

That is no anticlimax. It is rather a revelation that the gospel in all its wonder, as well as its simplicity and tenderness, brings to us a salvation whose blessings are to be applied first and foremost in God's ideal for society—the home.

So all the tremendous truths of the early chapters of this letter—the eternal purpose of God, the sealing of His Spirit, the life of the Head in the Body—are focused on this one spot, that we might see the fruit of the gospel where it can best be generated to others—in the home.

We are reminded, therefore, that marriage is a divine institution. Indeed, the family is the first institution of society. God created man male and female, and said, "Therefore shall a man leave his father and his mother, and shall cleave unto his wife: and they shall be one flesh" (GENESIS 2:24). Therefore His plan for marriage demands that it be monogamous and permanent. All developments such as bigamy, polygamy and polyandry violate this standard. As part of the principle of occupation of the land, God commanded, "Neither shall he multiply wives to himself, that his heart turn not away" (DEUTERONOMY 17:17). Wherever that principle is broken, you have misery and sin.

Some people assert that marriage is an institution of the state, but the Christian viewpoint is that it is antecedent to the state. There was no state when marriage was instituted. When two people come together in wedlock it is before God and under God. He may not have been the impelling motive in every case, but He stands behind every marriage, for marriage is the heart of the social order.

Attacks on the family are aimed at the fundamental order of things as established by God, and Scripture says that violators, fornicators and adulterers will be judged by God. Because society condones violation of the marriage law, that does not mean a man escapes the judgment of God.

The state which permits separation of families on trifling grounds commits a great crime and destroys its very foundation, for history proves that the society which treats the marriage relationship lightly inevitably decays.

All theories aganist the permanence of the family, whether communistic, socialistic or the product of free thought, are pernicious. We are dealing with that which is a key matter in the moral order of the universe.

But we have talked *about* this passage of Scripture: it eagerly waits to speak for itself. Let us try to gather together its teaching.

1. *The Pattern of Marriage.* Here I think the key word is "Saviourhood." How are husband and wife to think of each other in their home life from day to day? Certainly with consideration, affection and devotion. But what is to be the inspiration of this? They will never think quite fully of one another unless they recognize that their relationship one to another is intended to follow the pattern of that which exists between Christ, the heavenly Bridegroom, and His church, which is His bride.

(a) *Verse 23.* Christ is Head and Saviour of the church. He is sovereign. The church is subject to Him in everything: His authority over her is complete, for she is ruled and governed by Him. When we become members of His body by our new birth, we are no longer our own: we belong to Him, and we find that in submission to His will and authority as Head, we enjoy His love and experience His protection. That is what the word "Saviour" means here: *Provider, Defender, Protector.* He cares for us, meets our every need, and provides for us as His bride.

(b) *Verse 25.* Christ loved the church and gave Himself for her. That is the exact word Paul used in Galatians 2:20 concerning his own relationship to the Lord: ". . . who loved me, and gave himself for me." Yes, it is wonderful to know His love for us personally, but His purpose in dying was to call out a people to Himself to be His bride.

So we measure the love of Christ for His people by the fact that He loved us so much that He died for us—the supreme example of self-sacrificing love.

(c) *Verses 26-27.* His love intended our perfection, our complete cleansing. Of course, you can't put the word "bride" and the word "dirty" in the same sentence. He cleanses us and washes us by His Word, and we are justified by faith in Him alone. Then He purifies us and makes us holy, that in heaven He might have a perfect bride, delighting in her as His own treasure. And though we may fall short of that here, yet the love of Christ in our hearts makes us yearn for Him and for His will, that we may not be ashamed when we see Him. His love has our sanctity as its goal.

(d) *Verse 30.* As members of His body, we share a community of life. Our spiritual life had its source in His death. Just as Eve was taken out of the side of Adam, so the church was taken out of the wounded side of Christ, and through trust in Him we are His and made partakers of His nature. Such is the wonder of our salvation.

Here, then, is the pattern for marriage: sovereignty, sacrifice, sanctity and salvation. How is it to be expressed in daily life?

2. *The Power of Marriage.* The key word is "submission." It is with that word in verse 21 that the theme is introduced, and this is the word which is to be the power behind every Christian marriage.

(a) *Verses 22 and 24.* There is no suggestion here of mere authority on the one side and mere submission on the other. Children are to obey their parents (6:1), but that is a very different word from the submission of wife to husband. There is no suggestion that a selfish, tyrannical husband has a right to the submissive obedience of his wife in all things. Nor that a wife who refuses to yield her own will has the right to the self-sacrificing devotion of her husband.

The submission of the wife to the husband is as unto the Lord (v. 22). It is part of her relationship to Christ. In Him there is neither male nor female, but leadership is given to the man (GENESIS 3:16). Eve had overstepped her bounds when she yielded to Satan, giving evidence that she should not be free, but rather subject to her husband and dependent on him. This subjection was the result of the display of her own weakness, and Paul emphasizes this in I Timothy 2:11-14. This is not to suggest that the husband is in any way superior to the wife, but the submission of the wife is a God-given arrangement and part of her obedience to the Lord. A body with two heads is a monstrosity. A church with two heads cannot prosper. A home with two heads cannot stand.

The wife's submission is for her own protection and provision, and therefore the husband's relationship to the wife is one of love and self-sacrifice. Just as the pattern of the heavenly relationship is submission of the church to Christ, so it is the love of Christ to the church. When a husband loves his wife as Christ loved the church, there is no problem about submission. A man whose love is as free from selfishness as was the love of Christ finds a wonderful response in a love from his wife who is truly and only satisfied with such authority. For the authority of husband over wife is not that of domination, but of sacrifice.

How easily this can be forgotten, and everything taken for granted. Occupied with earning a living, facing severe competition in business, the husband may use his home as a restaurant or a dormitory and take love for granted. Not only does he court the one of his choice, but the two should be lovers always (v. 25). The word for love is *agape*, and it is the same kind of love that took Jesus to Calvary. The love that is "forbearing and kind, that knows no jealousy, does not brag, is not conceited, is not unmannerly nor selfish, nor irritable, nor mindful of wrongs. The love that is full of hope, full of trust, full of endurance. The love that never fails" (1 CORINTHIANS 13:4-8, *Weymouth*). Here is the pattern for the husband: he need never fear loving his wife too much, or telling her too often that he does! Here, then, is the pattern expressed in the power of marriage: submission; love. What a wonderful reward will follow, for just as Christ delights in the beauty and perfection of His people, so the love of husband for wife, and the submission of wife to husband— the loving self-sacrifice of each for the other—develops the personality of both and reflects the loveliness of the love of Christ to others. Christian marriage is the greatest factor for spiritual development.

3. *The Permanence of Marriage.* The key word here is "sanctity" (v. 30-31). When God made a woman He took her not from the head of Adam, lest she should dominate him, nor from his feet, lest he should dominate her, but from his heart, that there might be mutual love. "Therefore shall a man leave his father and his mother, and cleave to his wife: and they shall be one flesh." This is in accordance with the pattern of our relationship with Christ. He died for us, lives for us, gives us His nature in a love which is everlasting. Could we ever imagine Him to be unfaithful?

How, then, can we speak of divorce? What God hath joined together, let not man put asunder! Marriage is a union for life between one man and one woman. Every-

thing less than that is a perversion. The marraige relationship is exclusive. Even as our loyalty and allegiance are
toward one God, so with every husband and wife. Believe
me, though a country or popular opinion may sanction
"free love," God will surely judge it.

What am I to say to the home where things are in tragic
contrast to all of this? Through unwisdom of conduct,
want of frankness, a willful clinging to their own ways, a
refusal to accept the discipline which marriage exerts,
through violence of temper or neglect of common courtesy, estrangement has come in, respect has weakened,
love has worn away and bitter antagonism has sprung up:
the marriage is on the rocks.

I can only say that we must go back to the place where
God was left out, where the principles and pattern of
Christian marriage were forgotten. That may mean beginning all over again for some who have never known the
sanctity of marriage and its spiritual significance. Even
though the worst has happened, God can forgive and restore and make that home even yet a corner of heaven.
Remember the word of Christ to the woman taken in the
act of destroying the sanctity of her home and character,
when she came to Him, acknowledging Him as Lord:
"Neither do I condemn thee: go, and sin no more" (JOHN
8:11). Yes! Begin again just there—an acknowledgment
of the Lordship of Jesus—and watch Him begin to
work.

And finally, to those who would rush into such a relationship lightly, remember Matthew 6:33. Let Him
choose for you the one of His choice. You will be far
happier unmarried than married out of the will of God.

8

THE MINISTRY OF THE HOLY SPIRIT

ACTS 1-2

There is no teaching in the Bible about which we find so
much muddled thinking as that of the Holy Spirit. I think
the least understood day in the Christian calendar is
Whitsunday. I wonder how many readers know when
Whitsunday really is? Let me enlighten you a little. The
word *pentecost* means "fifty days"; and in the Acts of the
Apostles (1:3) we read that, following the resurrection of
our Lord from the tomb, He was "seen of them forty
days." Then there came a ten-day prayer meeting after
His ascension, and if you add forty to ten you have fifty,
and you arrive at the Day of Pentecost, which we call
Whitsunday, and which is always observed fifty days after
Easter. Good Friday, when Jesus died, was the fulfillment
of a great portion of Old Testament prophecy; but Pentecost was the fulfillment of the promises of the Lord Jesus
which He gave us in the Gospels.

Many questions are asked about the Holy Spirit. Who is
He? What is He? Whom does He indwell? What does He
do? What is meant by the fullness of the Spirit? Can a
Christian lose the Holy Spirit? What is meant by quench-
ing the Spirit? It is quite impossible, of course, to deal
with these in one message. But there is one principle
which I want to underline and to illustrate from the Word
of God. It is this: The action of the Holy Spirit in and
upon your life depends upon one thing, and one thing
only, and that is your attitude toward the Lord Jesus
Christ. There are four possible attitudes you may take

concerning the Person of God's Son: you may resist or reject Him; you may trust Him; you may yield to Him; and you may obey Him.

Notice the reaction of the Holy Spirit to these attitudes: you reject Christ, the Holy Spirit convinces of sin; you trust Christ, the Holy Spirit enters your life and begins to indwell; you yield to Christ, the Holy Spirit immediately fills the yielded heart; you obey Christ, the Holy Spirit begins to use the obedient life.

The action of the Holy Spirit always and immediately corresponds to the attitude of the heart toward the Saviour. These are not two; they are one. The Holy Spirit convicting is, in fact, Jesus Christ knocking at the door. The Holy Spirit filling your life is, in fact, Jesus controlling the yielded life. The Holy Spirit using your life means that He is carrying out the will of Christ because you are obedient. So, you see, there are four possible attitudes toward Christ that any of us can take, and they are immediately responded to by four possible actions of the Spirit of God.

In the New Testament you read of the disciples being filled with love, or filled with fear, or filled with joy. That doesn't mean that there was no room at that particular moment for any emotion other than love or fear or joy. It does mean that at that time love or fear or joy was on top and in control. When a man is filled with the Spirit of God, it does not mean that he is oblivious to any other emotion, but it does mean that he is controlled and mastered by the Lord Jesus Christ, who is on top in every area of his life.

Let us look at these four attitudes to Christ and the four actions of the Holy Spirit. Let us see them operating in the New Testament, and especially in the Book which we call the Acts of the Apostles (but which should really be called "the Acts of Holy Spirit Through Yielded Men.")

The Holy Spirit has never been withdrawn from the church. Dr. A. W. Tozer said, addressing several hundred ministers, that there are hundreds of churches from which the Holy Spirit could depart at any minute and nobody would ever know. That was a shattering statement. The Spirit of God has never been withdrawn from the Christian church. He is there, indwelling the heart of every Christian, every believer; but there are hundreds of professing Christians from whom He could withdraw and nobody would notice any difference.

> God's great gift to the church was Pentecost.
> God's great weapon for counteracting sin was Pentecost.
> God's great counterattack against all the powers of evil is the Spirit-filled Christian.
> God's great answer to the need of your life is a real experience of the Holy Spirit.

What attitude are you taking toward Jesus, and therefore what action is the Holy Spirit having upon you?

The first possible attitude toward Christ is that of *rejection;* and if you reject Christ, then immediately the Holy Spirit convinces of sin. Read Acts 16, the familiar story of the Philippian jailer, and Acts 24, the story of Felix the judge. Both of these men had rejected Jesus Christ. Both of them listened to the Apostle Paul preaching. Both of them were convicted of their need. The Philippian jailer comes in, shaken by an earthquake, and says to Paul, trembling under a spirit of conviction: ". . . what must I

do to be saved?" (16:30). The judge Felix also trembled
as he listened to the testimony of the same man. We read
that, as Paul reasoned with him concerning judgment,
temperance and self-control, Felix trembled.

I wish God would give to me constantly a ministry that
would at least make people tremble; that there might be a
ministry of such authority from my life and from my lips
and from my heart, coming from the very throne of God,
that would make people tremble as I would reason with
them concerning self-control, judgment, temperance! As
the Apostle Paul reasoned with him, Felix trembled; but
he said: ". . . when I have a convenient season, I will call
for thee. Go thy way for this time" (24:25).

Both of these men, I repeat, rejected Christ. Both of
them listened to the message of the gospel. One of them
said, "What must I do to be saved?" The other went on
resisting and said, "At a more convenient season I will call
for you." Both of these men, because they rejected Christ,
came under the conviction of the Spirit of God, and trembled.

It is the ministry of the Holy Spirit, and of Him alone,
to do this. A man's conscience will convince him it is
wrong to break the law, but only the Spirit of God operating through the prayers of God's people—and remember,
a prayerless congregation always means a powerless
pulpit—brings into a man's life the consciousness that the
greatest sin of all sins, for which there is no forgiveness
unless it is repented of, is rejection of Jesus Christ.

If you are unsaved, thank God for any measure of conviction that may be upon your heart now because you
have rejected Jesus; don't trifle with it. I would give to
you this solemn word of warning: if you turn a deaf ear to
the voice of the Holy Spirit, your ear will soon become

spiritually deaf and unable to hear a thing that God would say to you. You cannot be saved when you like. You cannot come to Christ when you choose. You can only become a Christian when God likes; and God likes right now. His time is always *now*. He never promises tomorrow. I repeat, therefore, to reject Jesus Christ is immediately to bring into your life the conviction of the Holy Spirit, even perhaps to the point of trembling—and even at that point you may go on rejecting. It is a great thing when a man begins to tremble; when he becomes conscious as God would reason with him concerning temperance, self-control, judgment to come; when he recognizes that there is a God to whom he will have to answer one day.

Our first attitude toward Jesus, therefore, is rejection; and the immediate action of the Holy Spirit is to convict. But when a man turns to Christ, then the Holy Spirit enters the *trusting* life and begins to indwell. The very personality of the Godhead begins to live within this bit of human clay that is your body. Remember the stab of conviction that struck the congregation when Peter preached the gospel on the day of Pentecost: they were "pricked in their hearts" (2:37). This was the fulfillment of the promise of the gospel that when the Holy Spirit would come, He would convince the world of sin. On the day of Pentecost He came, and a man began to preach in the power of the Spirit and the people were pricked, convicted, in their hearts. This was the immediate action of the Spirit of God upon that congregation: they were stabbed by conviction. What was Peter's answer to it? It was this: *Repent, believe the gospel, and you shall receive the gift of the Holy Spirit.* The promise was in John 7:38, 39. Jesus said, "He that believeth on me, as the scripture hath said, out of his belly shall flow rivers of living water. (But this spake he of the Spirit which they that believe on him should receive . . .)."

The new birth—that tremendous miracle that is an absolute necessity if we are to enter the presence of God; that encounter with deity that makes it possible for God to forgive sin on the basis of the cross of Jesus Christ—is absolutely impossible except for the operation of the Spirit of God upon your life. Jesus said, "It is the spirit that quickeneth; the flesh profiteth nothing" (JOHN 6:63). "Except a man be born of water and of the Spirit, he cannot enter into the kingdom of God" (JOHN 3:5). The Apostle Paul takes up the theme in Romans 8:9: "Now if any man have not the Spirit of Christ, he is none of his."

The entrance of the Spirit of God into the life of a man is spoken of in Scripture as the baptism of the Holy Ghost. "There cometh one . . . after me," said John the Baptist; ". . . he shall baptize you with the Holy Ghost" (MARK 1:7 8). The message of the risen Christ in Acts 1:5 was: ". . . ye shall be baptized with the Holy Ghost not many days hence." Every believer has the Holy Spirit. You do not pray to receive the Holy Spirit. You receive Him who was outpoured at Pentecost by trusting Jesus Christ as your Saviour.

That is breathtaking! The Spirit of God actually poured out at Pentecost is here—not floating in the atmosphere, but actually resident in the life of every believer. That is what makes a church service dynamic and revolutionary, capable of changing a human life for evermore. That is what makes a church service different from any other kind of meeting under the sun. God is in the midst; and perhaps if we realized that, we would behave differently and listen more carefully. If we realized that, we would tremble more frequently and disobey less often. We would crawl under our chairs and say, "O God, be merciful to me a sinner!"

The outpouring of the Spirit of God, expressed in the life of a child of God, is the means by which a man who is an unbeliever or a backslider may come right back again through the convicting power of the Spirit into a life of blessing and victory. We are not here to have fun and games, or to entertain people, or merely to try to persuade others to have an interesting evening in church. We are here to plead that they might get right with God. We should have a deep concern in our hearts that our church might see revival; and it will only do that when people inside it mean business with the Holy Spirit.

You do not ask to receive the Holy Spirit, but you trust Jesus Christ; and in that act of trust He comes to live within and indwell you. Oh, the mighty outpouring of the Spirit of God, the potential power that is available to your heart now, if only you trust in Christ!

Have you ever trusted Christ and committed your life to Him like that? Trust Him to bear your burdens and your guilt, to cleanse you from sin, and to come and live within you by His Spirit. Oh, what a miracle could take place in your heart right now!

The third attitude toward Jesus is to *yield* to Him; and as soon as you do so, the Holy Spirit's action is to fill. While every Christian has the Holy Spirit, not every Christian is filled with the Spirit. That is why there are verses like Ephesians 5:18: ". . . be filled with the Spirit." And the fullness of the Spirit—God's purpose for your life—the overwhelming power of the Spirit of God comes in answer to your yieldedness. Don't talk about surrender too much; that is a military term. Yieldedness is a family word. A child doesn't surrender to his father; he yields. That is not oppression or domination, but love, tenderness, the response of the heart, and a glad, happy yielding to the father and mother. What a happy home it is when there is that spirit of yieldedness, but what a miserable business when it is enforced surrender!

When our attitude is to yield to the Lord Jesus, then the Holy Spirit fills in an action of love. At Pentecost, all of them were filled. In Acts 4:31, we read that they were all filled again, and the place was shaken where they were gathered together when they prayed. I'd love to be in a meeting like that! They were filled to overflowing, yet the next chapter begins with an ominous word, "but." It is the first "but" in the Acts of the Apostles, and you know you are in for trouble when there is a "but"! Ananias and Sapphira lied to the Holy Spirit. They kept back part of the price of their land. They were not filled because they were not yielded; they were only playing the hypocrite because they had pretended to be yielded and they were not. They pretended that what they gave was everything. They have plenty of reproductions today: people who pretend to give everything, but don't, people who pretend to yield to the Lord, but don't; therefore they are not filled or yielded, and the Holy Spirit has never acted by coming into their lives in fullness.

When John Mark deserted in his first term of missionary service at Perga, he was not filled or controlled by the Spirit. Demas went back because, as Paul says of him in II Timothy 4:10, he "loved this present world." Poor fool! He chose to love this world, and you always do that which you love most. Demas went to Thessalonica, and do you know what sort of folk he met there? ". . . certain lewd fellows of the baser sort" (ACTS 17:5). Sure, they are always waiting! A man who does that is not filled with the Spirit because he is not yielded to Jesus Christ.

There were four men in the Acts of the Apostles of whom it is said that they were filled with the Holy Ghost. Each of them was wholly yielded to the Lord, and the results are most interesting.

Acts 4:8: "Then Peter, filled with the Holy Ghost said unto them, Ye rulers of the people and elders of Israel . . . ," and then he went on preaching. He was yielded to Christ, filled with the Spirit, and he immediately received power to witness.

Acts 6:5: ". . . they chose Stephen, a man full of faith and of the Holy Ghost . . . ," and one day he was stoned to death. He was a man yielded to Christ, and therefore filled with the Spirit, given power to suffer for Jesus.

Acts 11:24: Barnabas "was a good man, and full of the Holy Ghost and of faith: and much people was added unto the Lord. . . ." He was yielded to Christ, therefore filled with the Spirit, and he was used to win others for the Saviour.

Acts 13:9: "Saul, . . . filled with the Holy Ghost, set his eyes on him, and said, O full of all subtilty and all mischief, thou child of the devil, thou enemy of all righteousness, wilt thou not cease to pervert the right ways of the Lord?" This man was yielded to Christ, filled with the Spirit, and he had power over the devil.

Do not look at these things as mere theory. Think of them as your solemn responsibility in the sight of God and before heaven, in the light of the outpouring of His Holy Spirit. Think of your responsibility, for which you will have to answer in eternity if you fail to avail yourself of it. A man filled with the Spirit has power to witness; a man filled with the Spirit has power to suffer; a man filled with the Spirit has power to win other people; a man filled with the Holy Spirit has power to overcome the devil. I would suggest to you that those are the four things you need most in your life.

Let us be done with the deception of Ananias and Sapphira! Let us be done with the desertion of John Mark! Let us be done with the backsliding of Demas! Let us be yielded to Christ and be filled with the Spirit and have power in all these areas! Our third attitude toward the Lord Jesus, therefore, is yieldedness; and in response to that yieldedness immediately there is the Holy Spirit's action of filling.

There is one other possible attitude toward Jesus Christ that a man may take: Christ is *obeyed,* and the Holy Spirit uses. ". . . the angel of the Lord spake unto Philip, saying, Arise, and go toward the south . . ." (ACTS 8:26). God commanded and Philip obeyed. In verse 29, God speaks to him again and says, "Go near, and join thyself to this chariot"—*I want to use you!* Philip obeyed and was used by the Holy Spirit.

Again, in Acts 10:15, a voice had spoken to Peter and now "the voice spake unto him again the second time, What God hath cleansed, that call not thou common." Here the Lord was seeking to overcome prejudice against the Gentile world in the sight of Peter. Notice Peter's obedience (v. 21): "Peter went down . . ."; (v. 23): "Peter went away . . ."; (v. 27): "He went in. . . ." He did exactly what God told him to do; and finally, "While Peter yet spake these words, the Holy Ghost fell on all them which heard the word" (v. 44). God commanded him, Peter obeyed, and the Holy Spirit immediately used him.

In Acts 9:6, Paul, on the road to Damascus (as he met his risen Saviour), said, "Lord, what wilt thou have me to do?" The Lord told him what to do, and he obeyed. In

Acts 13:2, the Spirit of God said, "Separate me Barnabas and Saul for the work whereunto I have called them." So God commands, Paul obeys, and the Holy Spirit uses.

Here, then, we see something of these principles worked out in the Acts of the Apostles. Now I would apply it to your heart and life, for your attitude toward Jesus Christ determines the action of the Holy Spirit in your heart.

Let me ask you a pointed question: What attitude, right now, are you taking toward the Lord Jesus Christ? Are you resisting Him? If so, the Holy Spirit has been convicting you of sin unless you have resisted Him so long that you have become—tragedy of tragedies—spiritually deaf. What are you going to do about that? Has your attitude been to trust Christ? Then immediately He has come to indwell, and the miracle of the new birth takes place. How gladly the Holy Spirit goes into action and begins to indwell!

Have you yielded your life completely to Christ? Then, in answer to that yieldedness, immediately the Holy Spirit acts and fills. Are you willing to obey Jesus Christ without question, without reserve? Then, for the first time in your life, perhaps, the Holy Spirit will begin to use you.

As I think of the mighty outpouring of the Spirit of God, I realize the great power that is operative, and can be operative, within the life of every Christian, and the tremendous things that could happen through the church if only our attitude toward Jesus Christ were right. I know that the Spirit of God has been acting in every one of our lives, either in conviction, or in entering, or in filling, or in beginning to use. What action has the Spirit of God been able to take? That all depends upon what has been your attitude toward the Saviour.

Remember that your body is the temple of the Holy

Spirit if you are a Christian, and you are not your own; you are bought with a price. He lives within you and has the right to possess, to use, and to own you. One day you are going to stand before a holy God, to give an account of the things done in your body. I would not like to face Him and know that the whole outpouring of the Spirit of God was made available for me, personally, and yet I resisted and turned my back upon it because my attitude toward Jesus was not right, and therefore God could not use or fill, but had to put me aside on the shelf, and my life became barren, dead and futile.

9

CHRISTIAN WARFARE—ENEMY TACTICS

. . . now on whom does thou trust, that thou rebellest against me?—ISAIAH 36:5

Each of us, as a Christian, is engaged in daily warfare. The Apostle Paul reminds us that "we wrestle not against flesh and blood, but against principalities, against powers, against the rulers of the darkness of this world, against spiritual wickedness in high places" (EPHESIANS 6:12). The Christian is against something. It is not popular today to be against something, but that is the Christian's position. Our awareness of the devil's existence is sometimes rendered very dim simply because of the shallowness of our commitment to the Lord Jesus. Satan does not have to bother about us; and furthermore, the spiritual defeat which, alas! so often occurs in our life is largely due to an ignorance of the strategy of the enemy.

The language of the text quoted above is the gauntlet which Satan flings at the feet of anyone who dares to break out of his clutches and start walking along the Calvary road. I want to expose something of the method of the enemy of souls, not only from the Word of God, but from bitter personal experience which I trust will bring blessing and comfort to all who read.

The context of Isaiah 36 relates the story of King Hezekiah, who began to reign as King of Judah when he was twenty-five years old. His father was probably the worst king the nation had ever known, and he practiced all manner of idolatory. He was ultimately overcome by his enemies, because the country was spiritually rotten and in such a condition yielded to panic in the face of the strength of the opposition. In a final attempt to ward off defeat, King Ahaz had emptied God's house of all its treasures, and had given them to the Assyrians. Finally he closed the doors of the house of the Lord to worship, and instructed the people to worship the gods of the enemy so as to gain their favor. Never had Judah been reduced to such a low position; and at that moment Hezekiah began his reign.

During the early years of Hezekiah's reign, the Assyrian army attacked Israel, overcame it, and took captive the ten tribes—from which captivity they have not yet returned because they had refused to obey the voice of God. Now only the little nation of Judah was left, and in a desperate plight spiritually and morally. Hezekiah might have given every excuse to claim the position was hopeless, but spiritual revival always breaks out when things are at their lowest ebb, and he began his reign by opening the doors of the house of the Lord and cleansing it from the filthiness that had accumulated in it.

We are closed up to the grace of God for all spiritual blessing that we should receive. There is one thing we can do, however, and that is open the door of the house of the Lord. In that most familiar of New Testament texts, which is almost always used as the basis of an evangelistic appeal, but which is in fact addressed to a church, we read, "Behold, I stand at the door, and knock; if any man hear my voice, and open the door, I will come in to him, and will sup with him, and he with me" (REVELATION 3:20). Where God's house is shut, the lamp of testimony has gone out, prayer is a thing of the past, Bible study ceases to exist, and uncleanness accumulates. Is that true now in your life? If so, it is time to open the door of your heart to Him.

Following the cleansing of the temple and the renewing of the offering for sin, there began to be the song of the Lord once more in Judah. How fresh and vital and thrilling is the experience of God! There is the new song that springs from the heart; may we always know it in its freshness, and never lose its spontaneity and power, because it is the joy of the Lord which is our strength in the spiritual battle.

Therein we have a picture of things that were happening in Hezekiah's time: a church (Christian, if you like) revived, refreshed, cleansed, awakened. And that is the priority need for our day. Immediately upon his accession to the throne, Hezekiah challenged the whole nation to turn to God. The lamentable thing in this decade is that the church has no voice: it never speaks out on any subject. It is afraid, and because of fear it compromises. It is never heard where it ought to be heard, nor does it speak with authority. Of course, there is a sense in which it dare not be heard, because the only church which dares to raise its voice in authority is the church that has experienced spiritual revival. The only Christian who can raise his or her voice in testimony to win another for Christ is the man or woman who is living in the joy and blessing of salvation.

We are told that many messengers whom Hezekiah sent through the land were laughed to scorn, but a great multitude humbled themselves and came to Jerusalem to spend fourteen days in communion with God. Their voice was heard, and their prayer came up to His holy dwelling place in heaven, and the outcome was that the whole country experienced a flame of revival. Every idol was torn down, and before long the country turned from sin and idolatry and became humbled and dependent upon

God. It happened because one man refused to lie down before the threat of the enemy.

It takes just one man in high authority to raise his voice, regardless of what it may cost him, to turn the course of history in any country. Would to God that might happen! I tremble to think of what will happen to nations unless they experience a spiritual awakening.

Revival, however, is God's sovereign gift. But you can live in it personally and experience it day by day in your heart and life, as the writer of this hymn says:

> The dearest idol I have known,
> Whate'er that idol be;
> Help me to tear if from Thy throne
> And worship only Thee.

Far too long our Christian lives have been two-faced, and our testimony has been negative and ineffective. Oh, that God would make us real, through and through!

But what about the enemy? It was against this background of spiritual revival and awakening that he struck with relentless force. We have seen a revived worship, a humble people—*then came Sennacherib!*

My friend, it is *then* that God tests the reality of our determination to be wholehearted. Your heart has been opened to Christ; the song of the Lord has been heard again through your life; the desire to send out the challenge and to spread the Good News to others has been implanted; you have sought to destroy every idol and determined to be all-out for God: *then—the devil!*

This is his chance. As I have said, he never had to bother about you before, as you were no problem to him; but now you are a danger to his fiendish plans to outwit

God's purposes. You know nothing of the wiles of the devil until you are out-and-out for God and for souls. The measure of his concern about you is governed by the measure of your abandonment to the Lord. People hate the terms "full surrender" and "absolute commitment," but they are the only terms of the New Testament. The moment these become your personal experience, then comes the enemy.

Now for his exposure. In the fourteenth year of Hezekiah's reign, Sennacherib—no doubt well aware of what had been going on, but somewhat skeptical because he had heard about reformation and turning over a new leaf many times—took the fenced cities of Judah (ISAIAH 36:1). The next verse tells us that he then set out to attack Jerusalem, but between verse 1 and verse 2 we must know what Hezekiah's reaction was to the capture of so much outlying territory. That was a test for him! The enemy had obtained a foothold in his land, and danger threatened. In II Kings 18:14 we read that Hezekiah sent to the King of Assyria, saying, "I have offended; return from me: that which thou puttest upon me will I bear." And he gave him all the silver in the house of the Lord, and cut off all the gold from the doors of the temple.

Hezekiah, what came over you? We can hardly believe what we read! After all the cleansing of the house of God, at the first spiritual test we see you fail.

Let us see where he failed: Hezekiah sent to Sennacherib, who had not yet threatened Jerusalem, and met him halfway, saying, "I have offended." That was a lie, because the Lord was with Hezekiah and he prospered wherever he went. He was willing to come under bondage again, to bear whatever Sennacherib put on him, even after tasting spiritual victory. Further, he took the treasures out of the house of the Lord; he was willing to give the sacredness of his love and the secret of his power to the enemy.

The effect of his compromise was to invite another attack, this time on the citadel itself (ISAIAH 36:2). Compromise never thwarts Satan's attacks; it merely guarantees that he will make another one. Notice that the enemy had begun with the outer country. Had he begun with Jerusalem, the very urgency of the situation would have driven Hezekiah to the Lord. Satan always begins with the little things, and once he sees a loophole given him by compromise, he launches a large-scale attack upon the heart and life.

"Don't trouble about your quiet time this morning—you're too hurried." "Never mind missing your Bible reading for one day—you can read it again tomorrow." "This is not the moment to speak to your office colleague about Christ—you had better keep quiet or you will be misunderstood and only do harm."

Have you heard these insinuating whispers from the enemy? Time and time again he begins to whisper into the ear of the child of God. Resist him in the name of Jesus at the very outset, and you have won the battle. Once you start on the policy of compromise, believe me, you will be brought to the very depths of humiliation before you experience the hand of God laid bare to deliver you.

Satan makes you panic at times of pressure; he will get you frantically busy so that you have no time for Bible study or prayer. He will get you discouraged with the opposition of your family or friends so that you are inclined to throw in the sponge, and say it isn't worthwhile. And so he takes the fenced cities.

On his second invasion the enemy's tactics are to attempt to capture the throne. Sennacherib questioned the basis of Hezekiah's confidence: "What confidence is this wherein thou trustest?" (ISAIAH 36:4). So the enemy attacks faith as the foundation of all outward courage. The Assyrian king would not have dared to do that at the beginning of his invasion, but once he had Hezekiah yielding on little things, he attacked him at the very center.

Once Satan has made you close your Bible for a few days, and silenced your prayer time and your witness, then he begins to attack your faith. "On *whom* are you trusting?" And you are inclined to say to him, as Hezekiah said, "I'm sorry, but I don't really know." You have lost the basis of your confidence. It is wonderful to recall at such a moment the man Peter, who was attacked like that, who went on denying his Lord until he broke down and wept bitterly, and then heard Christ saying to him, "I have prayed for thee, that thy faith fail not . . ." (LUKE 22:32).

The enemy said (v. 6), "Are you trusting in Egypt? If so, Egypt is a broken reed." At that point he was right (Satan does not always tell lies). In verse 7 the Assyrian poured scorn on Hezekiah, saying, in effect, "If it is God you are trusting in, well, you have cut down all the idols, and therefore you have cut off the source of His power: all the outward show of your religion is gone." God, however, knew what had happened in the heart of Hezekiah to cause him to abolish idolatry, even if the enemy was ignorant on that point.

Even worse, Sennacherib claimed to be coming in the name of the Lord (v. 10). What arrogance! Yes, so often Satan comes as an angel of light, speaking to our hearts of his good intentions. Then the Assyrian came up with an agreement (v. 16). Satan always wants that! But there can never be any agreement between God and the devil, and for us to attempt it is fatal.

The ultimate of Sennacherib's attack was to suggest that, in reality, his service was much better than that of Jehovah (v. 17). He promised better conditions for the people and boasted of his power, telling of previous victories. Alas, unhappily that was true! I am sure, if we are honest, we can recall occasions of utter defeat, of which Satan reminds us—here, and there, and there again—and we have to admit he is right. In doing so he questions the power of God. Sennacherib insinuated that if the gods of other nations proved futile to help the people, how could the people of Judah expect their God to assist them? That was the height of his attack, and it was the ultimate of blasphemy. Eventually, that is what Satan seeks to do: to claim to be a greater and more powerful force than Jehovah.

How often Satan whispers, "It's not worth it: Jesus cannot help you. I'm more powerful than He, so why bother trying to carry on against such opposition?" When you are in a situation where prayer and Bible reading have been neglected, then you are no longer sure of your ground, and you do not know where you really stand, and you find to your horror and dismay that Satan has not only acquired the fenced cities, but has also attacked the heart.

Notice Hezekiah's twofold reply, and see how he had learned his lesson: ". . . they held their peace, . . . for the king's commandment was, saying, Answer him not" (v. 21). In the face of such a torrent of abuse, Hezekiah knew that he was absolutely helpless. To argue or dispute would have been a waste of time. He could have referred to the mighty hand and stretched-out arm that had brought the people of God out of Egypt, but no good ever comes of argument or discussion with the devil. Let God shut his mouth, for you cannot. The greatest of all authority for that attitude is demonstrated by the Saviour Himself, who, in the face of the most bitter attack hell ever made upon heaven in the Person of Jesus Christ, ". . . as a sheep before her shearers is dumb, so he openeth not his mouth" (ISAIAH 53:7).

Not only did Hezekiah refuse to answer the enemy, but he rent his clothes, covered himself with sackcloth, and went into the house of the Lord (ISAIAH 37:1). Here is a testimony to his indignation at the contempt poured upon the name of God, and to his own absolute dependence upon Him for deliverance. As Hezekiah went before the Lord that day he was saying, in effect, "Lord, it does not matter much what happens to me; that is only secondary. But Your glory is at stake in this issue. And only God can defend His own honor.

When Satan challenges you, "In whom do you trust, that you rebel against me?" there is only one resource in such a circumstance. It is to go before the Lord, cast yourself upon Him, and claim His defense of His honor in your life. It is the power of the Holy Spirit within you which leaves Satan baffled, beaten and in complete despair. Go now, if you are suffering defeat, and claim the mighty power of the blood of Jesus to be your defense against the warfare of the enemy.

10

CHRISTIAN WARFARE—
THE SECRET OF VICTORY

*Knowing this, that our old man is crucified with
him, that the body of sin might be destroyed, that
henceforth we should not serve sin—*ROMANS 6:6

Do you often wonder why it is that so many of us, as
Christians, are slow to reveal any evidence of spiritual
growth? Why is it that we live so long in defeat? Why is it
that there is so little ringing, clear-cut testimony to victory over sin? Why do these things happen, with the result that we are often disillusioned about the Christian
life?

When we were converted we imagined everything
would be clear sailing, and we would find we had no more
problems with sin. We had entered into the reality of
"There is therefore *now* no condemnation to them which
are in Christ Jesus . . ." (ROMANS 8:1); we had received
forgiveness, and we were free from sin. But subsequent
years have proved this view of sin a fallacy, for while
assured of forgiveness, we found ourselves engaged in a
battle that was too much for us, and our testimony has
been silenced. We have had nothing to say about Jesus as
Saviour simply because we have had no real experience of
deliverance from sin. Why should these things be?

I am sure the answer to that question has to be found if
we are ever to recover the ringing note of certainty in our
testimony. Dr. Graham Scroggie used to say, "Too many
Christians live on the right side of Easter, but the wrong
side of Pentecost; the right side of pardon, but the wrong

side of power; the right side of forgiveness, but the wrong side of fellowship. They are out of Egypt, but they have not reached the land of promise and blessing, and are wandering about in the wilderness of dissatisfaction and frustration."

This is not a side issue; I am not dealing with a subject which is irrelevant to these days of crisis. We must find the way whereby the church can recover her lost power and vitality and once again become a dynamic force which can sweep through all the opposition and the materialism of today with conviction and authority. This can be done only by believing people who are enjoying full salvation. What, therefore, is the reason for defeat, and what is the way out of it?

Personally, I am convinced that the reason for it is that we have never really appreciated the full significance of the cross. We are tremendously concerned about experiences of the Holy Spirit these days, but the thing we surely need to remember is that the first and supreme work of God the Holy Spirit in the Christian is to glorify the Lord and point him to Christ as the risen Lord. Therefore, that is what we should now seek to do—to look again into His face and see what He has done for us, and therefore can do in us every day. It is not a question of going on to Pentecost, but back to Calvary; then Pentecost is inevitable.

A defective view of the atonement is always due to a defective view of what sin really is. Romans 6 in no uncertain terms gives the definition and spells out the true character of sin. We have no space to consider this chapter in detail, but let us concentrate on verse 6: "Your old evil desires were nailed to the cross with Him" (*Living Letters*).

DELIVERANCE FROM SIN EXPLAINED

We see in Romans 6:6 that the subject Paul is dealing with is much more than sinful acts: it is the principle of sin itself, which exists in all of us by nature—Sin with a capital S, the old self, a tyrant and a rebel, all that man is apart from the grace of God.

All of us have found it comparatively easy to understand that the Lord Jesus was wounded for our transgressions and bruised for our iniquities, that He died for our sins on the cross, and that as we receive Him as our Saviour we have forgiveness full and free. But somehow that has not dealt at all with sin as a principle. We see that the cross has dealt with the *fruit,* but not with the *root;* with *sins,* but not with *sin;* and unless we understand this other aspect of the meaning of Christ's death, we simply cannot help going on sinning, for we have no resources that can prevent us from doing so. Surely God has done more for us at Calvary than to give Jesus to die for the *fruit* of our rebellion, and simply to offer forgiveness of sins, wonderful as that is. Certainly He would not consider having a family of children who are still rebels. The cross has struck at the very heart of our rebellion against His authority, which, of course, is at the root of sin. Our old man is *crucified with Him,* says the Scripture.

In his masterly book *The Law of Liberty in the Spiritual Life,* Evan Hopkins says, "Christ's death, which has separated the believer from the *consequences* of sin as a transgression, has also separated him from the *authority* of sin as a master, and set him free. The believer sees that Christ, by dying for Him, has completely delivered him from the *penalty* of sin; so it is his privilege to see that because he was identified with Christ in that death he is also delivered from Sin as a ruling principle: its *power* is broken. He is in that sense free from sin, and the cross is the efficient cause of this deliverance; freedom from sin's ruling power is the immediate privilege of every believer. It is the essential condition or starting-point of true service as well as real progress. Such service and growth are as possible for the young convert as for the mature believer. Therefore freedom from sin's dominion is a blessing we may claim by faith just as we accept pardon. We may claim it as that which Christ has purchased for us, obtained for our immediate acceptance. We may go forth as set free from sin and as alive unto God in Jesus Christ our Lord."

This is freedom from sin as a ruling principle: we may enter in by faith to an experience of deliverance from sin's tyranny as vital and real as at our conversion, when we received Jesus Christ as our Saviour and entered into the joy of forgiveness of all our sins. Deliverance from sin, as well as forgiveness of sins were provided at Calvary, but most of us for years of our Christian life have settled for a half-salvation.

DELIVERANCE FROM SIN ESTABLISHED

Romans 6:6 (*Living Letters*) goes on to say, ". . . that part of you that loves to sin was crushed and fatally wounded, so that your sin-loving body is no longer under sin's control. . . ."

But, you say, these old desires that have been nailed to the cross are always with me, and I am very conscious of them. If that part of me which loves to sin was crushed and fatally wounded, why is it that I am so conscious of its existence?

Now, let us think again about what Jesus did for us at the cross. Not only was He dying for sins, but that transaction which effected a complete forgiveness for our sins was accepted in heaven because it was based upon a life that He had lived in which He died to sin. Having died to sin as a principle in His life, He was able in His death to forgive sins. You remember that wonderful word of the Apostle Paul in Philippians 2:5-8: "Let this mind be in you, which was also in Christ Jesus: Who, being in the form of God, thought it not robbery to be equal with God; But made himself of no reputation, and took upon him the form of a servant, and was made in the likeness of men: And being found in fashion as a man, he humbled himself, and became obedient unto death, even the death of the cross."

What was Jesus doing? He was stepping down the ladder from glory to a manger in Bethlehem: He was living a life in which He forsook His rights and refused to act independently of the will of God. In Him there was no sin principle. He never rebelled; He always was submissive; and because that life of meekness and submission—against which all the powers on earth and hell fought Him tooth and nail, and to whom He never yielded an instant—was entirely and utterly a dependent life, He had died to the sin principle and condemned it in the flesh. He hung upon the cross as a condemned criminal, not only to forgive our sins, but as One who took to Calvary a nature that had never yielded to sin.

If I have claimed the benefit of a share and oneness in the death He died, in order that I might be forgiven, surely I can also claim a share in the life He lived, which He took to the grave in order that I might in Him know deliverance from the principle of Sin. If I can say, "He bore my sins in His body on the tree—thank You, Lord, hallelujah!" can I not also say that at Calvary He nailed every evil desire to the cross, and crushed and fatally wounded that part of me that loves to sin, so that this body of mine, this sin-loving body, is no longer under sin's control? That should also be part of my conversion experience, for the life that He lived and the death that He died resulted in His perfect humanity being raised to the throne. "Wherefore God also hath highly exalted him, and given him a name which is above every name: That at the name of Jesus every knee should bow, of things in heaven, and things in earth, and things under the earth; And that every tongue should confess that Jesus Christ is Lord, to the glory of God the Father" (PHILIPPIANS 2:9-11).

Death had no power over Him, and having received from the Father the gift of the Holy Spirit, He imparted at our conversion His nature in which He had triumphed over every temptation to sin. We receive at our new birth a life in which there is no rebellion and no sin principle, and He has come to dwell within each one of us to make that real in our everyday experience.

So, you see, the experience of deliverance is a glorious liberty. It means that no longer do we try to improve the self-life; we have finished with it, for it has been nailed to the cross, and in its place we have all the resources and power of the life of the risen Lord Himself. How many of us have spent years on attempts at self-improvement, and just as many of us have found it utterly futile! God never planned for us to try to improve ourselves, or to make ourselves better, but He has planned that we be replaced by Jesus, and that we should by faith draw upon His life and power.

DELIVERANCE FROM SIN EXPERIENCED

But how does all this work out in experience in daily life? Look again at Romans 6:6: ". . . that the body of sin might be destroyed [made of none effect], that henceforth we should not serve sin." Or, as *Living Letters* states it: ". . . your sin-loving body is no longer under sin's control, no longer needs to be a slave to sin."

Professor Godet says of this chapter: "This is the divine secret of Christian sanctification which distinguishes it from simple natural morality. The latter says to a man, 'Become what you want to be.' The former says to the believer, 'Become what you are already in Christ.' It puts a positive fact at the foundation of moral effort to which the believer can return and have resource anew at every instant. This is the reason why his labour is not lost in barren aspiration, and does not end in despair. The believer is not disentangled from sin gradually; he breaks with it in Christ once for all."

Of course, this deliverance has no existence whatever apart from Christ Himself in us. Put a lighted candle into a dark room and the darkness disappears, but the tendency to darkness remains, and the room has to be maintained in a state of light by a continual counteraction of light to darkness. The law of the spirit of life in Christ is always in force, and we are always dependent upon it. This is the proof that the law of sin and death is not extinct, and the tendency to sin is still here. Never in this life are we free from the presence of sin. Apart from Christ as our indwelling Light, even the most mature Christian would at once relapse into a state of spiritual decay, because the law of sin would no longer be counteracted by the law of Christ. It is by His indwelling life that He sets us free from the law of sin, and counteracts the natural tendency to sin by the law of the spirit of life.

The only good thing about a Christian is Jesus. He is the opposite to all that you and I are by nature. We are conscious of our unholiness, but He is holy; we are conscious of our impurity, but He is altogether pure; we are conscious of our impatience, but He is patient; we are conscious of our lack of grace, but He is gracious.

Oh, what a joy to be able to lay hold of Him every moment, and therefore find that indeed this body of sin is made of none effect because the victorious life of the Saviour has become ours in daily experience! *In Christ* we are dead to sin, but sin is never dead to us. It is with us and in us always, and will overwhelm us if we fail to draw upon Christ's life.

The only holiness that the New Testament teaches is holiness by faith in Christ, by appropriation of the life of Christ and the power of Christ every moment of the day. Fail to yield and appropriate, and the Holy Spirit fails to work. He goes out of business, not out of your heart, but you relapse into a spiritual decay and defeat which make a mockery of so many years of Christian living. But you yield, and He works. Keep on yielding, and He keeps on working, and so in daily living you experience the dynamic power of the upward pull of the living, triumphant Lord overcoming the downward drag of a sinful nature.

You see, we are delivered from one slavery into another. Notice throughout Romans 6 how often the word "servant" is used:

V. 16: "Know ye not, that to whom ye yield yoursselves *servants* to obey, his *servants* ye are to whom ye obey. . . ."

V. 18: "Being then made free from sin, ye became the *servants* of righteousness."

V. 19: ". . . for as ye have yielded your members *servants* to uncleanness . . . even so now

> yield your members *servants* to righteous-
> ness. . . ."
>
> V. 20:   "For when ye were the *servants* of sin, ye
> were free from righteousness."
>
> V. 22:   "But now being made free from sin, and
> become *servants* to God. . . .'"

The Christian is a servant of Jesus Christ, and this involves a change of masters, a new sovereignty, a new
authority, a new dominion. Therefore, we are to yield ourselves to God, and our members as instruments of righteousness to God.

Let us face it honestly: Have we not for far too long
settled for a half-salvation, having received the forgiveness of sins, but knowing nothing of deliverance from the
sin principle? Perhaps we didn't know that it was provided for us at the cross, as was forgiveness. What a miserable experience it has been! How defeated we have
been! How lacking in reality and dynamic has been our
testimony! Would you make this moment one when you
not only claim by faith the *death* of Jesus to forgive your
sins, but also the *life* of the risen Lord to deliver you from
the sin principle? Just as you appropriate by faith the one,
so take by faith the other, and enter into a full salvation.

> My Saviour, Thou hast offered rest;
> Oh, grant it then to me,
> The rest of ceasing from myself
> To find my all in Thee!

That is what changes the Christian life from drudgery
to luxury, from a feeble sort of effort to believe what

doesn't seem to work into a radiant, glowing testimony to the power of the living Christ within you to do what you cannot do by yourself. Yield yourself to Him; strive no longer to improve yourself, but moment by moment take His life from above.

Just as you took the step of faith that led you to become a child of God as you believed in the cleansing power of His blood, now take the step of faith that will lead you into the land of full salvation. For it is when a Christian has died out to himself, ceasing to base any confidence in the flesh, reckoning that the whole of that self-life has been nailed to the cross—when he begins to lay hold of the life of Jesus, and knows the authority of the Holy Spirit upon him and the power of the living Christ revealed through him—that you have revival.

But you must tell the Lord you are willing to die. He must hear your assent and the readiness of your heart to what has already been accomplished at the cross: "I have been crucified with Christ." That, of course, goes right to the very heart of pride and self. It reduces you to the absolute minimum; but—praise the Lord!—it makes way for God by His Spirit to do in you His maximum.

11

GOD'S PROGRAM OF WORLD CONQUEST

Psalm 2

In this twentieth century which began, in the judgment of all who were living at that particular time, by ushering in what was going to be the golden age, two world wars have taken place which, in shattering that illusion, have prepared the way in a most amazing manner for the fulfillment of prophecy in two specific areas.

The First World War released Palestine from the rule of Turkey and opened the way for the return of the Jews —an event which, you will remember, took place just a few years ago, shortly after the Second World War. In Ezekiel 37:21 there is clearly indicated the trend of prophecy along the line of the gathering of the scattered Jewish people from all the nations of the world back into their homeland; and now, for the first time since A.D. 70, there is a nation of Israel.

One of the most amazing things in history is the way in which the Jews have been preserved as a people. That could never have happened to any other people. For any other nation to be defeated, persecuted, slaughtered and scattered as Israel has been would have meant the extermination of their national life. Not so with the Jews. God has protected and preserved His ancient people, as He said He would.

Again, these two world wars prepared for the emergence of two great world confederacies, which are clearly depicted in prophecy. The first of them, the northern confederacy, is led by the Soviet Union, which until the First

World War was largely an area of ignorant, uncivilized and uneducated people who were a liability more than an asset to the Allies in 1914-18. But now a great power has emerged in Russia, and we have seen the amazing development of this great northern confederacy. From Ezekiel 38:1-4 and 39:1-4, we see quite clearly that Russia heads this northern confederacy; yet she can never attain world dominion.

I do not believe that there will be a nuclear war between Russia and America. I know it is very dangerous for any preacher to say that, but I risk such a prophecy because I am quite convinced, for Scripture teaches it, that Russia's interests are in the amazing wealth of the Middle East, Palestine, Iran, Suez—all these lands rich in resources, rich in oil, rich in minerals. Her concern for America at this moment, of course, is that America is too powerful for her to dare to take the risk and make a grab at the coveted prize; and so her goal, I believe in the United States is to watch that country weaken from within. That is why she has a very conveniently placed ally only a few miles off the shore of America. When Russia makes the grab for Palestine, and she surely will as prophecy is fulfilled, she will take the risk at God's moment; and at that moment America will be so weakened by moral collapse and racial problems that she will have no power to retaliate.

We see in Scripture, therefore, the ultimate, inevitable overthrow of Russia, because God is against her. Daniel 2 tells us that another confederacy will emerge in the later days, and that is the western confederacy, of which we suggest that NATO (North Atlantic Treaty Organization) forms the basic elements. We are going to look at various parts of prophecy, and I want you to follow me carefully and prayerfully. I do not want to tickle your mind, or to give you some new theories, but I trust in the authority of the Spirit of God to warn and to prepare your hearts for things that must surely come.

In Daniel 2 we have the account of Nebuchadnezzar's amazing dream of a great image, with its different values in terms of its head, thighs, legs, and so on. And Daniel, giving the interpretation of this image to Nebuchadnezzar (v. 38-40), indicated that in his dream Nebuchadnezzar had a complete vision of world history, and had seen the emergence of four kingdoms. His own kingdom was the first, Babylon; this was to be replaced by Medo-Persia; Medo-Persia by Greece; and Greece by Rome; and there would be no more kingdoms until the Lord should come.

Let us look now at this western confederacy, because the indications and the teaching of prophecy are that the northern confederacy, headed by the Soviet Union, will be in direct opposition and conflict with the western confederacy, headed by the antichrist, which will be in shape a re-formed and revised Roman Empire.

The dream indicated (v. 41-45) that in the last days this empire will consist of ten kingdoms, made up of the ten toes of of this gigantic image. It will be ruled over by ten kings, in quality like a mixture of different philosophies and different forms of government, unified one day by the emergence of a great political figure, sometimes called "the beast," sometimes called "the man of sin," as described in Revelation 13. One day, in the days of those kings (DANIEL 2:44), shall the God of heaven set up a Kingdom. This is when God is going to intervene. He shall set up a Kingdom which shall never be destroyed; in other words, there will be no more kingdoms. And the Kingdom shall not be left to other people, but it shall break in pieces and consume all these kingdoms; and it shall stand forever.

Let us pause to remind ourselves again of the amazing accuracy of prophecy, that there have only been four world kingdoms since that time. It would naturally be supposed that, with the collapse of the Roman Empire, another would emerge to take its place, but none other has. There have been many attempts on the part of many people to achieve world power, and this is why I am very conscious of my need of care in speaking upon these subjects. I remember a book that was published in Britain during the war by an expert on this theme—which I confess I am not—a minister who was regarded as the outstanding prophetic preacher of our day, and who proved quite conclusively, at least to his own way of thinking, that Mussolini was none other than the man of sin. You see, it is very dangerous when you get involved in the details of this kind of situation.

Many people have imagined themselves to be the one who should emerge to control world power; nobody has done it. But in the day of the revival of the Roman Empire, and in the day of these kings, the God of heaven Himself will set up a Kingdom which shall never be destroyed. "Forasmuch as thou sawest that the stone was cut out of the mountain without hands [that is, without human ingenuity, or planning, or organization, or ability, *without hands*], and that it brake in pieces the iron, the brass, the clay, the silver and the gold; the great God hath made known to the king what shall come to pass hereafter: and the dream is certain, and the interpretation thereof sure" (DANIEL 2:45).

The stone cut out without hands—there could be no

doubt as to the one to whom this refers: it must be the Lord Jesus. Many times in Scripture He is referred to as the Stone; the Rock upon which He will build His church; ". . . the stone which the builders disallowed, the same is made the head of the corner; . . . a stone of stumbling, and a rock of offence" (1 PETER 2:7-8). This is the Lord Jesus; there could be no possible misunderstanding here, and "the stone that smote the image became a great mountain, and filled the whole earth" (Daniel 2:35).

Man's interest through the centuries has always been in the image. Every effort has been made by politics, by science, and, in many areas, by religion to keep this image on its feet. At any cost this great colossus must be kept standing. Everything must be done to keep world government stable. I am not given to attacking from the pulpit people, or things, or situations, or religious movements. I would rather be positive in my preaching than be against things. But one of the dangers of the ecumenical movement is its pronouncements along this line, and here is one of them, just recently: "The church's primary responsibility is to consider the development of productive, stable and just economic institutions." I do not find that in my Bible. This is not the church's priority task at all. Of course, I do recognize that the gospel has social implications, and we are in great danger of neglecting them. But here, you see, is the teaching that every effort must be made in order to keep this image standing. Man's interests are in the image. God's interests are in the Stone. And one day this Stone, cut out without hands, shall cut into the image—not gradually bringing about its collapse, but cutting into it, grinding it to powder, smashing its authority—and will assume total world government.

What is God's program in order to bring this about? Do not let us get any fanciful interpretations here. As I have suggested to you, this is going to happen in a day when the Roman Empire is to be revived under the antichrist. I have not time to go into this in detail, but the number of nations mentioned here in Daniel are found in three places at least in prophecy. Here they are in the dream of Nebuchadnezzar's image. You find them again in Chapter 7, which is a prophecy that falls into line with the second and deals with the beast who has ten horns; and you find the same thing again in Revelation 13, where you have the picture of the man of sin (antichrist) with ten crowns. So here is the final form of world government, and Scripture tells us that there is nothing in it that will honor or recognize God. Everything in it will honor and deify and recognize man.

I read from Revelation 13:16: ". . . he causeth . . ."—this is the antichrist, this leader, this great head of final world government—"all, both small and great, rich and poor, free and bond, to receive a mark in their right hand, or in their foreheads: And that no man might buy or sell, save he that had the mark, or the name of the beast, or the number of his name." The whole philosophy of humanism will find its ultimate expression in the worship of man as God. Study the map of Europe, consider the European Common Market, the division of Germany into West (a part of the Roman Empire) and East (never a part of the Roman Empire), and see it all taking shape. Paul states in II Thessalonians 2:3-4: "Let no man deceive you by any means: for that day . . ."—that is, the day of Christ—"shall not come, except there come a falling away first, and that man of sin be revealed, the son of perdition; who opposeth and exalteth himself above all that is called

God, or that is worshipped; so that he as God sitteth in the temple of God, shewing himself that he is God." I repeat that the whole philosophy of humanism, about which we see so much and with which we are constantly surrounded, is going to be brought to its climax when one man, having the rule over ten nations, assumes the place of deity, blasphemes the name of God, and declares that he is god.

The language of the Second Psalm in this connection is very significant. As we see what God is doing, and what God will do in the fact of these tremendous, shattering events that are to take place around us: "Why do the heathen rage, and the people imagine a vain thing? The kings of the earth set themselves, and the rulers take counsel together, against the Lord, and against his anointed, saying, Let us break their bands asunder, and cast away their cords from us." Here you see open rebellion. Here is open war. Here is the human heart coming out into the light and taking its place, the natural mind at enmity against God. Incidentally, you may know of the existence of an organization called the Four A's, the American Association for the Advancement of Atheism. This association operates under charter in New York State right now, and you could find its offices in New York. A recent publication of this society states: "We undertake to abolish public chaplaincies, to tax church property, to repeal Sunday legislation, to abrogate all laws enforcing Christian morals, to stop bootlegging of religion into schools, to prevent the issuing of religious proclamations by government officials, to erase superstitious inscriptions which deface our coinage, for there is no god, and our supreme effort will be to free mankind from the fear of a nonentity." This society operates today under charter.

Never have people been so defiant of authority, so bold in attack of any standard of decency. "Let us break their bands asunder! Let us cast away their cords from us!" And so the rulers take counsel against the Lord and against His anointed. And they seem to have plenty of confidence that they are going to do it.

There is only one thing that prevents the complete letting loose of hell on earth, and that is the presence of the church. "When he that letteth," says II Thessalonians 2:7-8—when he that hindreth is taken away, then hell will literally be let loose. And it may well be that the arrogant confidence expressed in this Second Psalm by the raging of the nations was inspired by the fact that, at the moment, everything that hinders the outburst of total wickedness has been removed and taken to heaven. And therefore, it would almost seem that Satan has won the day. "He that sitteth in the heavens shall laugh" (PSALM 2:4). That is a frightening word. What a contrast between the raging of world powers and laughter of God upon the throne!

There is no crisis in heaven. Unquestionably the war is on, and hell has declared war upon heaven. And in the day when antichrist rules, it will be fought to a finish. Why, asked the psalmist, do the heathen rage and the people imagine a vain thing? Why, indeed? Why, after all that God has done? Why, after all the demonstrations in love? Why, after a cross and an empty tomb? Why, after the coming of Jesus, do the heathen rage? What have they against Him? The answer is very simple. It is a desire on the part of man, at last finding expression unhindered, to have his own way about everything, and God's Way about nothing. It is human nature inspired by the powers of darkness, literally expressing itself and revealing the wickedness of the human heart. And He that sitteth in the heavens shall laugh. The laughter of God in the Bible is a very solemn subject, for God only laughs in total derision. It is the laugh of omnipotence. It is the laugh of absolute authority. It is the laugh of total confidence in ability to destroy all totalitarian world power. He will not only laugh; "Then shall he speak unto them in his wrath, and vex them in his sore displeasure" (v. 5).

One day the world is going to meet a God of judgment, a God who is determined by virtue of the holiness of His character to stamp out sin, a God who must do it if He be God at all. At that day, before Him every knee shall bow. "Yet have I set my king upon my holy hill of Zion" (v. 6). See the contrast at this point between His first coming and His second. When Jesus came to Bethlehem, to Calvary, He came to die in our place. When he comes a second time, He will come to judge the man who is unrepentant. When He came the first time, He came to seek and to save that which was lost. When He comes the second time, He will come to judge all who know not God, and they shall be cast into a lost eternity. When He came the first time, He came to be our representative before the God of grace and love. When He comes the second time, He will come to be God's representative before a race of rebels whom He must condemn. When He came the first time, He came in great humility. When He comes again, He will come in great glory. He came first as a lowly Nazarene; He will come again as King of kings, Lord of lords. He came the first time wearing a crown of thorns; He will come again wearing a crown of glory. He came to be despised and rejected; He will come again and before Him every knee shall bow, and every tongue confess that He is Lord. He came riding a lowly ass; He will come riding a great white horse and leading the armies of heaven in His train. He came that He might in humility submit to earthly rulers. When He comes again He will compel the submission of every ruler to His authority. He came to shed His precious blood. He will come again as a mighty Conqueror with His vesture dipped in blood. What a contrast between His first and second coming!

When will this be? The great conflict that will take place between the western and the northern confederacy is known in Scripture as the Battle of Armageddon, when, without doubt, nuclear war will break out. Not between Russia and America—that could never be. If Russia and America got involved in nuclear warfare, there would not be any room for the fulfillment of any prophecy, because that would be the end of civilization. God will not let it happen like that.

Nuclear war will only happen in this world, I believe, in this total release, unhindered by the presence of the church, of what man really is by nature; and this tremendous battle between the northern confederacy and western powers, under the authority of the man of sin, will be in a contest centered around Israel. At that moment the Lord shall be revealed from heaven with fire and with great glory. All of these events will take place, I believe Scripture teaches, within a period of about seven years and will be known as the Great Tribulation.

But there is one other prophecy at which I must ask you to look as we see the unfolding of this program of God's conquest. Because the question is: Where do you and I come in, and what is going to happen to us? In Daniel 9:22-27 we read of another dream and its interpretation. Daniel had a tremendous vision, and it had baffled him, forcing him to his knees before God. He did not understand it; and as he was praying and confessing his sins, the angel Gabriel spoke thus to him: ". . . he informed me, and talked with me, and said, O Daniel, I am now come forth to give thee skill and understanding. At the beginning of thy supplications the commandment came forth. . . ." Incidentally, not to digress, but is that not lovely? When Daniel began to pray, God began to work. At the beginning of his supplications, the commandment came forth. How eager God is to speak to His people! ". . . and I am come to shew thee; for thou art greatly beloved: therefore understand the matter, and consider the vision. Seventy weeks are determined upon thy people and upon thy holy city, to finish the transgression . . ."—notice *to finish the transgression, to make an end of sins*—"and to make reconciliation for iniquity, and to bring in everlasting righteousness, and to seal up the vision and prophecy, and to anoint the most Holy. Know therefore and understand, that from the going forth of the commandment to restore and to build Jerusalem unto the Messiah the Prince shall be seven weeks, and threescore and two weeks . . ."—sixty-nine altogether—" . . . the streets shall be built again, and the wall, even in troublous times. And after threescore and two weeks shall Messiah be cut off, but not for himself: and the people of the prince that shall come shall destroy the city and the sanctuary; and the end therefore shall be with a flood, and unto the end of the war desolations are determined. And he shall confirm the covenant with many for one week: and in the midst of the week he shall cause the sacrifice and the oblation to cease, and for the over-spreading of abominations he shall make it desolate, even until the consummation, and that determined shall be poured upon the desolate."

Here is a man in great distress. He has prayed, and God

has brought him an interpretation of his prayer. God is revealing to Daniel what is His plan for His people Israel, and He says there will be a time of seventy weeks to be given to them (v. 24) when all His dealings and all of prophecy will be completed. That is seventy periods of seven years. Now, if it is seventy periods of seven years, this is a period of 490 years over which God is going to deal with the Jews and to finish all prophecy, and to bring in the consummation of the age. A period of 490 years that will commence, you notice, from the going forth of the commandment to restore and build Jerusalem. That means at the very moment when the King of Persia, Artaxerxes, gave the command for the Jewish people to return to their land and rebuild the wall, sixty-nine weeks, says Daniel, will be fulfilled, and then the Messiah will be cut off. It was exactly 483 years from the giving of the command by Artaxerxes for the Jew to return from their Babylonian captivity until the day that Jesus died on the cross. From that date named in history until the moment that He was crucified was the exact period that Daniel foretold. That means, therefore, that there was another seven years in which God was going to deal with His people Israel.

If you interpret the whole Scripture together on this point, you will understand that between the conclusion of that sixty-ninth week and the opening of the seventieth was to be a lapse of time, a period which the New Testament calls the time of the Gentiles, the period of the church, the time in which you and I are engaged, in which the Jew momentarily is set aside because of unbelief, and God, no longer dealing with Israel, but holding them for a moment aside, is now not dealing with the world by nation, but He is dealing with men and women one by one, on the basis of the blood that was shed on the cross, and the redemptive power of Jesus Christ, that in these days He might call out from every nation, every kindred and every tribe a people to His name. That is what God is doing. This, of course, Paul understood perfectly clearly, and is the theme of Romans 10 and 11.

How long it will be between the moment when Jesus was cut off and God again takes up His dealings with the Jew at the period of that great tribulation, we do not know. But we do know that the end of this Gentile age will be marked by a great climax, which is the coming of Jesus personally for His people, that He might gather out from all who live on that day those who have trusted Him and loved Him. The only reason why He should keep the church out from that period of tribulation is because He bore our sins on the cross. He says, in Revelation 3:10-11, "Because thou hast kept the word of my patience, I also will keep thee from the hour of temptation which shall come upon all the world, to try them that dwell upon the earth. Behold, I come quickly: hold that fast which thou hast, that no man take thy crown."

I believe that the rapture of the church, as Scripture teaches, shall mark the climax of the age in which we live; and the following this intermission in which God has set aside His chosen people because of their rejection of Him, and has opened the Word and the plan of salvation to every nation and every kingdom in all the earth, then this Gentile age will terminate with that great climax. ". . . the Lord himself shall descend from heaven with a shout, with the voice of the archangel, and with the trump of God: and the dead in Christ shall rise first: then we which are alive and remain shall be caught up together with them in the clouds, to meet the Lord in the air: and so shall we ever be with the Lord" (1 THESSALONIANS 4:16-17). That is the signal for our deliverance from this civilization which is rotten. It is the removal of "that which hindereth." It is the signal for the emergence of that final world government extending, as Daniel 9:27 teaches, into the first half of that tribulation period. It will be the signal, too, for the Lord to come with His angels, with His people, and cut into the image, to bring world domination to an end; and the Lord Jesus shall begin to reign.

The scriptures said of the Jews that they will look upon Him whom they have pierced, and they shall mourn because of Him (ZECHARIAH 12:10); He shall pour upon them the Spirit of grace and supplication, the Jewish nation at last will recognize their Messiah, and a fountain shall be open to them for sin and uncleanness.

God's interests are in the Stone cut out without hands. Man's interests are in the image, in keeping it on its feet. Where are the interests of your heart and of your life? As we think of the tremendous drama unfolding before us—that no prophecy of Scripture, as far as I am aware, yet remains unfulfilled to permit the Lord to come for His people, that these things are at our very door, and the whole civilization in which we live is taking this final shape which Scripture said it would—are your interests in propping up the image, or are your interests in the Stone? There is one thing that God wants you to do, and that is to cut out of the image, get into the Stone and cut out your interest in the image. That demands cessation of your interest in a tottering civilization, except with one objective—to save men from a lost eternity. If I am ever on a sinking ship, which I hope I never will be, I would not spend two minutes polishing up the brass, I would not spend a second giving lectures on seamanship; my one job would be to save life. And my concern is to ask if there has been a moment in your experience when you have deliberately cut out of the image so that your interests are not there anymore. Have you been put as a living stone into Jesus, that you might cut back into the image in Jesus' name, and rescue souls that are perishing, for the glory of God?